Italian Cooking with Olive Oil

Italian Cooking with Olive Oil

Diane Seed

William Morrow and Company, Inc. / New York

To Alexander,
already a discerning *intenditore*,
and Max,
an enthusiast,
who still has it all to explore

Library of Congress Cataloging-in-Publication Data

Seed, Diane.
Italian cooking with olive oil / Diane Seed.—1st ed.
p.   cm.
Includes index.
ISBN 0–688–12788–6
1. Cookery (Olive oil)   2. Cookery, Italian.   3. Olive oil.
I. Title.
TX819.042S44   1995
641.6'463—dc20   94–46990
CIP

Printed in the United States of America

First Edition

1 2 3 4 5 6 7 8 9 10

BOOK DESIGN BY RICHARD ORIOLO

Acknowledgments

I would like to thank the International Olive Oil Council for its help and support, and Fausto Luchetti and Irfan Berkan for their charming expertise.

Dennis Frith, Philippa Goodrick, and Arlene Wanderman have generously helped me when I have had second thoughts about some technical detail, and Professor Enzo Fedele clarified my thoughts about deep frying.

Friends in Italy always become involved when I am writing a book, and I would like to thank all those who helped eat the food, suggested dishes that must be included, and tried to keep me sane when the computer had tantrums, the cat insisted on howling, and everyday life in Rome became even more complicated than usual.

Special thanks to Dr. Antonio Capalbi, who puts up with it all, with varying degrees of good humor, and to my long-suffering family, who is tolerant when my cooking and conversation get fixed on a particular track.

Contents

Introduction

Italy is one of the world's largest consumers of olive oil,
and it would be difficult to imagine Italian cooking without this
vital ingredient. Olive oil is used in sautéing, deep frying, and
baking, and as a marinade or to dress salads, cooked vegetables,
seafood, and meat, and to add a crowning touch to soups
and bean dishes. Most pasta sauces would be
nothing without olive oil.

It would a great mistake and false economy, however, to use
the cheapest olive oil available. Each olive oil has its own
individual taste; one that gives a gentle flavor to a fish dish would

be inappropriate in a hearty bean soup. Italian cooks keep bottles of different olive oils in their larders, and choose them with as much care as the bottles in their wine racks.

For general cooking, almost any olive oil will do the job, but an extra virgin olive oil must be used for drizzling over a finished dish or anointing fish and vegetables. Of course, the better the oil, the better your food will taste.

Depending on the variety of olive in pressing, olive oil should be consumed within twelve to eighteen months of production. Store it in an airtight bottle in a cool, dark place.

At the end of each recipe, I have suggested an olive oil based on the classifications listed below along with recommendations of special regional olive oils. Search out and experiment with the many olive oils available so that you gradually develop your own olive oil palate. In Italy, every region, town, village, and family firmly believe that their olive oil is the best. You can have great fun deciding with whom you agree.

Classifications of Olive Oil

EXTRA VIRGIN OLIVE OIL

Extra virgin olive oil is obtained by pressing the fruit of the olive tree by mechanical and physical methods under controlled temperature conditions, which preserves the fruity flavor, color, and natural properties of the oil. By law, it must contain less than 1 gram free oleic acid per 100 grams.

Estate-bottled olive oils come from a specific geographical area and the name of the producer is usually found on the label. Sometimes, even the variety of olive is listed as well. The flavor of the oil may change from year to year depending on the variety of olive and variable weather and soil conditions. Use these oils sparingly as a finishing touch to your cooking or drizzled over vegetables, seafood, and other dishes.

Less expensive, popular blends of extra virgin olive oil are combinations of oils, often from many different olive-producing countries. All of them have less than 1 gram free oleic acid per 100 grams.

VIRGIN OLIVE OIL

Made by the same methods as extra virgin olive oil, virgin olive oils have more than 1 gram but less than 3 grams free oleic acid per 100 grams. These are not readily available in the United States.

OLIVE OIL

Once called "pure olive oil," this oil has a free oleic acidity of below 1.5 grams per 100 grams, but this is achieved by refining oils with a higher degree of acidity. Olive oil is suitable for deep frying.

"Extra light olive oil" also belongs in this category. The name is misleading because it is light only in flavor, not in fat or calories, making it ideal for deep frying sweet pastries.

Deep Frying with Olive Oil

In Mediterranean countries there is a long-established tradition of deep frying humble ingredients in olive oil to transform them into crisp, golden morsels of temptation. An old Ligurian proverb says *fritta é buona persino una scarpa,* "even an old shoe tastes good when it's fried."

When frying food in olive oil 60 percent of the moisture content of the food has to evaporate before olive oil begins to penetrate, while other fats penetrate more deeply into the food. This means food fried in olive oil has a crunchy texture and is less greasy than food fried in other fats.

GOLDEN RULES FOR DEEP FRYING

1. Use enough oil to get a satisfactory result. The amount varies according to the cooking vessel used for frying. If you are using an electric deep fryer, follow the manufacturer's directions. When using a pot, make certain it is deep enough to hold at least 2½ inches of oil.

Always heat the olive oil slowly until it reaches the desired temperature.

2. It is important that the oil maintains a constant temperature during frying. A moderate heat of 300°F should be used for dense, uncooked food such as chicken parts, large fish, or raw vegetables like artichokes. This ensures that the food is cooked through before turning too brown on the outside. A higher temperature of 325°F is necessary for food already cooked, or morsels dipped in batter or egg and bread crumbs. A temperature of 350°F should be used for very small pieces of food or tiny fishes. Olive oil begins to smoke at 435°F and the oil should not be allowed to reach this heat. Clip a candy/deep-fry thermometer to the side of a nonelectric pan to make sure the temperature remains constant.

3. Olive oil should be carefully filtered after each use through a paper coffee filter or a very fine mesh sieve. Store it in an airtight container away from light. According to experts it is safe to reuse the oil at least ten times before its nutritional properties are impaired. I prefer to use the same oil just three times.

4. Food that is fried should be slid gently into the oil, a few pieces at a time, to avoid cooling down the oil.

5. If more oil is needed, add it when a batch is finished cooking. Wait for the oil to reach the correct temperature before proceeding with the frying.

6. When the food is ready, lift it out with a slotted spoon, place it on paper towels to drain, and serve it at once. Fried food cannot wait around.

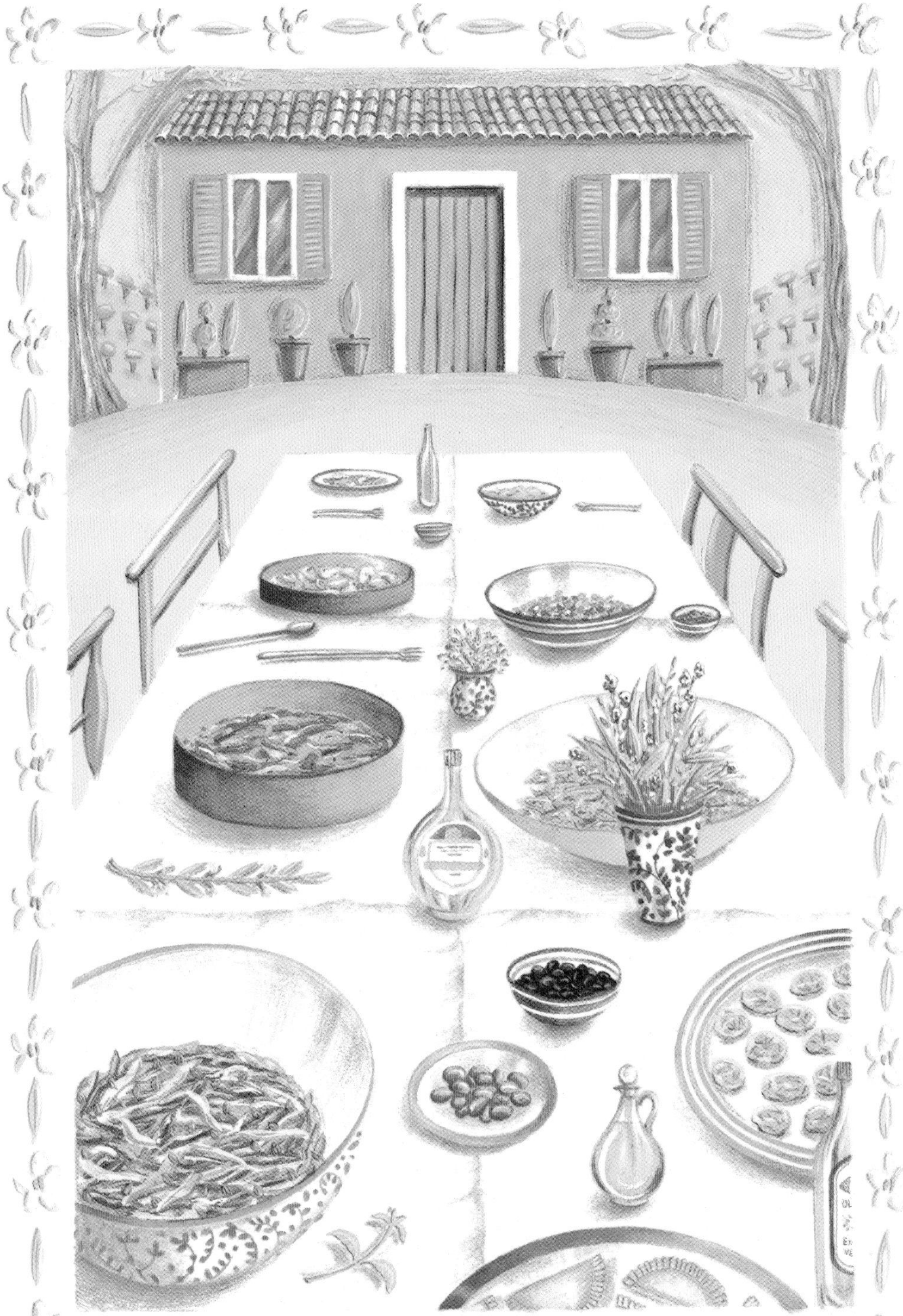

Antipasto

Antipasto literally means "before the meal," and all
kinds of delicious food can be found hiding behind this heading,
from the ubiquitous *prosciutto e melone* to assorted cold cuts,
vegetables preserved in olive oil, and crisp-fried tidbits. Many of
these antipasto recipes can be doubled or tripled to serve as a
main dish. The Italians elevated *l'arte di arrangiarsi* to an art form.
Copy their example and feel free to mix and match
as you develop your own menus.

❧

Summer Bagna Cauda

*B*agna cauda translates as "hot bath," and in the winter, this sauce is made with lots of butter and served hot as a dip. The warm-weather version is much lighter and healthier, and it is offered at room temperature. La Contea restaurant at Neive, in the Piedmont region, serves these roasted sweet peppers bathed in olive oil, anchovies, and garlic.

MAKES 4 SERVINGS

4 yellow or red bell peppers

¼ cup extra virgin olive oil, plus extra for brushing

2 garlic cloves, finely chopped, or more to taste

¼ cup chopped mixed fresh herbs, such as parsley, basil, chives, and/or marjoram

4 canned anchovy fillets, drained and chopped

Freshly ground black pepper to taste

Brush the peppers lightly with oil. Grill over hot coals or broil under a preheated broiler, turning occasionally, until the skins are blackened and blistered, about 10 minutes. Place in a paper bag and let sit until cool, about 15 minutes. Remove the stems, skin, and seeds, and cut the peppers into 1-inch-wide strips. Place on a serving platter. Using a mini-food processor or a blender, combine the garlic, herbs, anchovies, and the ¼ cup olive oil, and process to a smooth sauce. Pour the sauce over the peppers and grind black pepper over. Serve at room temperature.

Olive Oil Note: Use a light-flavored extra virgin olive oil.

Cheese Marinated in Spicy Olive Oil

FORMAGGIO FRESCO SOTT'OLIO

Small fresh cheeses are marinated in herbed olive oil both to preserve and to add flavor. Italians marinate local fresh cow's milk cheeses, but in America the tangier goat cheeses work just as well. If you can't find small cheeses, such as *crottins* or buttons, cut a log of goat cheese into one-inch-thick rounds. The herbs can be varied to suit individual tastes, as well as to use what's in the herb garden. Serve the cheese with bread and olives as an antipasto.

MAKES 8 TO 12 SERVINGS

4 small round fresh cheeses (about 3 ounces each)

6 large fresh basil leaves

6 large fresh sage leaves

2 small dried hot red chile peppers

12 black peppercorns

Approximately 1½ cups extra virgin olive oil

Fill a wide-mouthed 1-quart canning jar with boiling water and let stand for 10 minutes. Drain and dry with a very clean cloth. Place the cheeses in the jar, layering them with the basil, sage, chile peppers, and peppercorns. Pour in enough olive oil to cover the cheeses completely, adding more oil if necessary to cover. Close the jar tightly and refrigerate for 24 hours. To serve, remove the cheeses with a fork, letting the excess oil drain back into the jar. Store the cheeses in the refrigerator and use within 1 month.

Olive Oil Note: Use any extra virgin olive oil.

Preserving Sott'olio

*T*here is an ancient tradition of preserving everything from vegetables to fresh tuna under olive oil—*sott'olio*—especially in southern Italy. Olive oil covers the food in a closed jar, sealing off oxygen and preserving it for months. Some of Italy's best antipasti are prepared this way. Here are some guidelines for preparing *sott'olio* specialties:

Be sure the ingredients to be preserved are thoroughly dry. If they have been precooked in a wine or vinegar solution, drain them well and pat them dry with paper or clean kitchen towels. Some recipes ask for the ingredients to be drained overnight in a colander, and stirred occasionally, allowing them to dry thoroughly. A single drop of water can break the oil's seal, allowing air and bacteria into the jar, encouraging fermentation.

Air bubbles can also cause fermentation to occur. After covering the food with oil, let the jar stand until no more air bubbles come to the surface of the oil. Stirring the food in the jar with a chopstick or dinner knife will help release any trapped air bubbles.

If a recipe includes acidic ingredients such as wine or vinegar, the food will keep longer, because the acid discourages harmful bacterial growth. If the recipe doesn't include acid, the food will keep for less time—plan to eat it within a week or so, and watch carefully for any signs of fermentation, such as bubbling or a domed lid.

Before filling, wash the canning jars and lids with hot soapy water and rinse well. To sterilize, fill the jars with boiling water and let stand for 10 minutes. Drain and dry completely with a clean kitchen towel. Fill the jars while they are still warm.

The oil surrounding the food will solidify when chilled. Remove the jar from the refrigerator a few hours before serving to allow the oil to warm up and return to a liquid state, or place the jar in a bowl filled with a few inches of warm water to speed the process. Remove the food from the oil with a slotted spoon. Always add enough fresh oil to the jar to completely submerge the remaining food, as it must be immersed in order to remain preserved.

The refrigerator is the best place to store your *sott'olio*. In Italy foods preserved in oil are rarely refrigerated, but they are kept in cool, dark cellars—an area that fewer and fewer American homes have these days.

In any case, if you see indications of fermentation, such as bubbling or a domed lid, do not eat the food! Throw it away and make sure no human or pet can get to it.

Tiny Artichokes Preserved in Olive Oil

CARCIOFINI SOTT'OLIO

These are a great delicacy, but they can be prepared with only the very small baby artichokes found at specialty markets in early spring and fall.

MAKES 1 QUART

1½ cups white wine vinegar

1½ cups water

1 teaspoon salt

2 pounds small baby artichokes (about 18)

2 lemons, halved

12 fresh mint or basil leaves

Approximately 1½ cups extra virgin olive oil

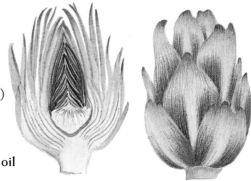

In a medium nonreactive saucepan, combine the vinegar, water, and salt. With a knife, trim the stem off 1 artichoke. Remove the tough outer leaves until the pale green center cone of tender leaves is revealed, and trim off the sharp tip of the cone. Rub the cut surfaces of the artichoke with the lemon halves to discourage discoloration. Pare away the thick green peel from the stem and base. Drop the trimmed artichoke into the vinegar solution. Repeat with the remaining artichokes. Set the pan over medium-low heat, bring to a simmer, and cook just until the artichokes are tender when pierced with the tip of a knife, about 12 minutes. Drain well and pat dry with clean cloth towels. Fill two wide-mouthed 1-pint canning jars with boiling water and let stand for 10 minutes. Drain and dry with a clean cloth. Layer the artichokes and mint leaves in the jars. Pour in enough oil to cover the artichokes completely. Let stand overnight, uncovered. Add more oil to cover the artichokes, cover tightly, and refrigerate for at least 24 hours. The artichokes will keep, refrigerated, for up to 1 month. Add more oil if necessary to cover the artichokes remaining in the jar as they are used.

Olive Oil Note: Use a full-flavored extra virgin olive oil.

Mixed Vegetable Antipasto

This makes an interesting pickle to serve with slices of cold meat or sausage. It can also be served as part of an antipasto table.

MAKES 1 QUART

1 pound carrots, peeled and cut into ½-inch cubes

2 medium white onions (about 8 ounces), chopped

2 celery ribs, cut into ½-inch cubes

½ cup chopped fresh flat-leaf parsley

½ cup packed fresh basil leaves, torn into small pieces

1 teaspoon salt

4 bay leaves

Approximately 2 cups extra virgin olive oil

In a large bowl, combine all the ingredients except the olive oil and toss well. Pour boiling water into a wide-mouthed 1-quart canning jar and let stand for 10 minutes. Drain and dry with a very clean cloth. Place the vegetables in the jar, and pour in enough oil to completely cover them. Let stand until no more air bubbles rise to the surface of the oil. Cover tightly and refrigerate for at least 24 hours. The vegetables will keep, refrigerated, for up to 3 days in all. Be sure to add more oil if necessary to cover the vegetables remaining in the jar as they are used.

Olive Oil Note: Use an extra virgin olive oil.

Marinated Eggplant Antipasto

While this is most often flavored with garlic and bay leaves, other herbs can be used—try fresh basil, oregano, or marjoram, or a combination. If you can't find small eggplants, cut three pounds of larger eggplants into one-inch cubes.

MAKES 2 QUARTS

1 bottle (750ml) dry white wine

4 cups white wine vinegar or white distilled vinegar

3 pounds small elongated Italian or Japanese eggplants (about 12), cut crosswise into 1-inch-thick pieces

2 garlic cloves, slivered

1 teaspoon salt

2 bay leaves (fresh or dried)

Approximately 3 cups extra virgin olive oil

In a large saucepan, bring the wine and vinegar to a boil over medium heat. Add the eggplant and cook until barely tender, about 5 minutes. Drain well in a colander. Place the colander on a plate and refrigerate, turning the eggplant occasionally, for 24 hours. Pour boiling water into two wide-mouth 1-quart canning jars and let stand for 10 minutes. Drain and dry with a very clean cloth. Layer the eggplant in the jars, sprinkling with the garlic and salt and adding a bay leaf to each jar when it is half-full. Pour in enough oil to cover the eggplant completely. Cover tightly, and refrigerate for at least 1 month. The eggplant will keep, refrigerated, for at least 2 months after opening. Be sure to add more oil if necessary to cover the eggplant remaining in the jar as it is used.

Olive Oil Note: Use an extra virgin olive oil.

Roasted Sweet Peppers with Capers and Oregano

Roasted peppers are one of the glories of the antipasto table. Red or yellow peppers work best, as green peppers can have a bitter edge after roasting.

MAKES 1 QUART

Approximately 1 cup extra virgin olive oil

4 red or yellow bell peppers, or a combination

1 tablespoon capers, preferably packed in salt, well rinsed and patted dry

2 tablespoons chopped fresh oregano

2 garlic cloves, slivered

½ teaspoon salt

Brush the peppers lightly with oil. Grill over hot coals or broil under a preheated broiler, turning occasionally, until the skins are blackened and blistered, about 10 minutes. Place in a paper bag and let sit until cool, about 15 minutes. Remove the stems, skin, and seeds, and cut the peppers into 1-inch-wide strips. Place on clean kitchen towels and let stand, turning often, until the surfaces are quite dry, about 4 hours. Pour boiling water into two wide-mouthed 1-pint canning jars and let stand for 10 minutes. Drain and dry with a very clean cloth. Layer the peppers in the jars, sprinkling with the capers, oregano, garlic, and salt. Add enough oil to cover the peppers completely. Let stand until no more air bubbles come to the surface. Cover tightly and refrigerate for at least 24 hours. The peppers will keep, refrigerated, for up to 3 days in all. Be sure to add more oil if necessary to cover the peppers remaining in the jar as they are used.

Olive Oil Note: Use an extra virgin olive oil.

Preserved Wild Mushrooms

Italians have a passion for wild mushrooms, which are often gathered from the damp forest floors as an autumnal family project. I do not recommend gathering your own mushrooms unless you are a trained expert, as many seemingly innocuous varieties are, in fact, poisonous. In North America, most consumers find their mushrooms in the market.

MAKES TWO 1 PINT JARS

2 pounds mushrooms, such as cremini, portobellos, chanterelles, or shiitakes, trimmed, stemmed if using shiitakes, and wiped clean with a damp cloth

6 cups water

3 cups red wine vinegar

2 teaspoons salt

10 black peppercorns

6 bay leaves

Approximately 2 cups extra virgin olive oil

If the mushrooms are very large, cut them into slices about ½ inch wide. In a large saucepan, combine the water, vinegar, and salt and bring to a simmer. Add the mushrooms, cover, and cook until just tender, about 10 minutes. Drain well and pat dry with paper towels. Pour boiling water into two wide-mouthed 1 pint canning jars and let stand for 10 minutes. Drain and dry with a very clean cloth. Layer the mushrooms in the jars, pressing them down as necessary to fit and sprinkling with the peppercorns and bay leaves. Add enough oil to cover the mushrooms completely. Let stand until the bubbles disappear. Cover tightly and refrigerate for at least 1 month. The mushrooms will keep, refrigerated, for at least 2 months after opening. Be sure to add more oil if necessary to cover the mushrooms remaining in the jar as they are used.

Olive Oil Note: The finer the olive oil, the better this elegant antipasto will be; use an extra-virgin olive oil.

Preserved Green Tomatoes

On the antipasto table these tart green tomatoes are an excellent foil for bland cheeses.

MAKES 1 QUART

3 large green tomatoes (about 1 ¼ pounds), cut into ⅓-inch-thick slices

½ teaspoon salt

Approximately 2 cups red wine vinegar

Approximately 2 cups extra virgin olive oil

Place the tomatoes in a shallow nonreactive bowl, sprinkle with the salt, and let stand at cool room temperature for 24 hours, gently stirring occasionally. Transfer to a colander and drain for 2 hours. Return the tomatoes to the bowl and add enough vinegar to cover. Let stand at cool room temperature for 24 hours longer. Drain well, and pat completely dry with paper towels. Pour boiling water into a wide-mouthed 1-quart canning jar and let stand for 10 minutes. Drain and dry with a very clean cloth. Pack the tomatoes in the jar (cut very large tomato slices into quarters if necessary). Add enough oil to cover the tomatoes completely. Cover tightly and refrigerate for at least 1 month. The tomatoes will keep, refrigerated, for at least 2 months after opening. Be sure to add more oil if necessary to cover the tomatoes remaining in the jar as they are used.

Olive Oil Note: Use an extra virgin olive oil.

Preserved Tuna

In the past, Sicilian fishermen enacted the *mattanza*, a bloody ritual slaughter of a tuna catch that supposedly originated with the Phoenicians as a sacrifice to the gods. (It is still performed in Favignana around the time of the summer solstice.) Huge portions of the fish were doled out to the attending families, and they preserved the bounty in olive oil.

MAKES 2 QUARTS

2 pounds center-cut tuna, in one piece

¼ cup coarse (kosher) salt

Olive oil to cover

Place the tuna in a large deep bowl and cover with cold water. Refrigerate, changing the water often, until the water remains clear, with no bloody traces, about 4 hours. In a pot large enough to hold the fish, combine 4 cups of water and the salt and bring to a simmer over medium heat, stirring to dissolve the salt. Add the tuna, reduce the heat to low, cover, and cook, turning occasionally, until the fish is opaque throughout when prodded with the tip of a knife, about 30 minutes. Place the tuna in a colander set on a plate. Refrigerate, turning occasionally, for 24 hours to drain. Fill two wide-mouthed 1-quart canning jars with boiling water and let stand for 10 minutes. Drain and wipe dry with a very clean towel. Pack the tuna in the jars and cover completely with olive oil. Place the jars in a canning rack in a large canning pot. Add enough water to cover by 1 inch. Bring to a boil over high heat, then cook for 10 minutes. Remove the jars from the pot and let stand at room temperature until cooled. Cover tightly and refrigerate for at least 1 week. The tuna will keep, refrigerated, for at least 3 months. Be sure to add more oil if necessary to cover the tuna remaining in the jar as it is used.

Olive Oil Note: My first choice is an olive oil from the south of Italy. Use regular or extra virgin olive oil, according to your budget.

Bresaola, Arugula, and Parmesan Salad

Bresaola (air-dried beef) is a delectable northern Italian specialty, found at good Italian grocers. This is one of my favorite starters, with the sharp, pungent flavor of arugula enhancing the air-dried beef.

MAKES 4 SERVINGS

4 ounces thinly sliced bresaola

2 tablespoons fresh lemon juice

⅓ cup extra virgin olive oil

Salt and freshly ground black pepper to taste

3 bunches arugula (about 1 pound) stems removed, well rinsed, and dried

1 ounce Parmigiano-Reggiano cheese curls (shaved from a large piece of cheese with a vegetable peeler)

Arrange the bresaola in a spoke pattern on four dinner plates. In a small bowl, whisk together the lemon juice, oil, and salt and pepper. Drizzle half the dressing over the bresaola. Arrange the arugula on the bresaola, and drizzle with the remaining dressing. Top with the Parmesan curls and serve immediately.

Olive Oil Note: Use a strong-flavored extra virgin oil, such as one from Umbria or Puglia.

Panzerotti with Olives and Onions

These golden brown deep-fried dumplings, with their heady tomato and olive filling, will disappear almost immediately from the platter. Every southern Italian region has a version of these, each with its own variation of filling. This one is from Puglia, the heel of Italy's boot.

MAKES 18

1 large baking potato (about 8 ounces), peeled

1 ½ teaspoons active dry yeast or 1 tablespoon fresh yeast

¼ cup lukewarm (105° to 110°F) water

3 cups all-purpose flour, or more as needed

Pinch of salt

¾ cup water, or more as needed

2 medium onions (about 8 ounces), finely chopped

2 garlic cloves, finely chopped

2 tablespoons extra virgin olive oil

3 ripe plum tomatoes, peeled, seeded, and chopped

1 cup Mediterranean black olives, pitted and chopped

Olive oil for deep frying

Cook the potato in boiling lightly salted water until tender, about 25 minutes. Drain, mash, and cool. You should have about 1 cup mashed potato. In a small bowl, sprinkle the yeast over the warm water and let stand until foamy, about 5 minutes. Stir to dissolve the yeast. In a large bowl, combine the flour, mashed potato, and salt. Stir in the yeast mixture, then stir in enough water to make a soft dough. Turn out onto a well-floured work surface and knead, adding more flour as needed, until supple and elastic, about 10 minutes. Transfer to an oiled bowl, turn to coat the dough with oil, and cover with plastic wrap. Let stand in a warm place until doubled in volume, about 1½ hours. Meanwhile, in a large skillet, cook the onions and garlic in the oil over medium heat until softened, about 5 minutes. Add the tomatoes and olives and cook until the tomato juices have evaporated, about 10 minutes. Remove from the heat and let cool completely.

To make the panzerotti, punch down the dough. Turn out onto a lightly floured work surface and knead briefly. Pinch off a piece of dough about the size of a golf ball (keep the remaining dough covered with plastic wrap as you work). On the floured work surface, roll the ball of dough into a 3-inch round. Place about 1 tablespoon of the filling in the center. Moisten the edges with water, fold over into a half-moon, and press the edges with a fork to seal. Place on a lightly floured baking sheet and cover with plastic wrap. Repeat with the remaining dough and filling. Preheat the oven to 200°F. Pour enough oil into a deep, heavy saucepan to come to a depth of 2 to 3 inches, and heat to 350°F over medium-high heat. (An electric deep fryer does the best job. Follow manufacturer's instructions for temperature.) Working in batches, fry the panzerotti, turning once, until golden brown, about 6 minutes. Using a slotted spoon, transfer to a baking sheet lined with paper towels and keep warm in the oven while you fry the rest. Serve immediately.

Olive Oil Note: Use any regular olive oil.

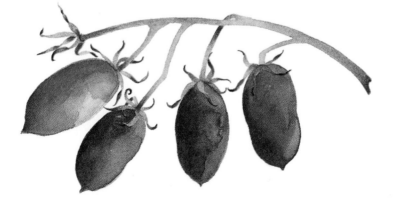

Yeast Fritters with Pizza Flavoring

These golden, savory puffs represent home cooking at its best. Traditionally, Pugliese families would serve them as a snack (or even supper) because they were easily made from pantry staples such as anchovies, capers, and olives. They are now prepared as a special treat for very good friends. I first encountered them at a dinner party in Lecce. A beautiful table was set in the dining room, but for the appetizer, we all trooped out to the kitchen, where *pettole* were fried up in front of us and served in all their simple glory. After this humble and delicious overture, we returned to the dining room for a more formal repast—but it's the *pettole* I still remember.

MAKES ABOUT 18

2½ teaspoons (1 envelope) active dry yeast or 1 tablespoon plus 2 teaspoons fresh yeast

½ cup lukewarm (100° to 110°F) water

3 cups all-purpose flour

A large pinch of salt, or more to taste

Approximately 1¼ cups water

3 ripe plum tomatoes, peeled, seeded, and finely chopped

1 small onion, finely chopped

¼ cup chopped pitted black Mediterranean olives

2 anchovies packed in salt, soaked in water for 1 hour, drained, filleted, and chopped, or 6 anchovy fillets packed in oil, drained and chopped

1 tablespoon capers, rinsed and patted dry

⅛ teaspoon crushed red pepper flakes

Olive oil for deep frying

In a small bowl, sprinkle the yeast over the warm water. Let stand until foamy, about 5 minutes. Stir to dissolve the yeast. In a medium bowl, combine the flour and salt. Add the yeast mixture, then stir in enough water to make a loose, sticky dough—almost a batter. Stir in the tomatoes, onion, anchovies, capers, and hot pepper flakes. Cover with plastic wrap and let stand in a warm place until doubled in volume, about 1 hour. Preheat the oven to 200°F. Pour enough oil into a deep, heavy saucepan to come to a depth of 2 to 3 inches, and heat to 350°F over medium-high heat. (An electric deep fryer does the best job. Follow manufacturer's instructions for temperature.) Drop heaping tablespoons of the batter into the hot oil, without crowding, and fry, turning once, until golden brown, about 5 minutes. With a slotted spoon, transfer to a paper towel–lined baking sheet and keep warm in the oven while you fry the remaining fritters. Serve immediately.

Olive Oil Note: Use any regular olive oil.

Broccoli Fritters

In Puglia, these fritters are made from many different vegetables; broccoli is one of the easiest and tastiest. If you and your guests are fans of bitter greens, use broccoli rabe when in season, in the autumn and winter.

MAKES 6 TO 8 SERVINGS

1 cup all-purpose flour

5 large eggs, beaten

A large pinch of salt, or more to taste

1 bunch broccoli (about 2 pounds) cut into florets, thick stalks discarded

Olive oil for deep frying

In a medium bowl, whisk together the flour, eggs, and salt until smooth. Cover and set aside in a warm place for at least 1 hour, and up to 4 hours. Preheat the oven to 200°F. Pour enough oil into a deep, heavy saucepan to come to a depth of 5 to 6 inches, and heat to 300°F over medium-high heat. (An electric deep fryer does the best job. Follow manufacturer's instructions for temperature.) Working in batches, dip the broccoli florets into the batter, carefully add to the hot oil, and fry, turning once, until golden brown, about 3 minutes. Using a slotted spoon, transfer to a paper towel–lined baking sheet and keep warm in the oven while you fry the remaining fritters. Serve immediately.

Olive Oil Note: Use any regular olive oil.

Zucchini Fritters

Just about anything tastes delicious dipped into this fluffy Neapolitan yeast batter and fried. (It also coats the Stuffed Fig Fritters on page 147.) In Naples, they stuff zucchini blossoms with mozzarella and anchovies, then coat them in batter and fry them. This recipe uses zucchini rounds as an easier variation.

MAKES 6 TO 8 SERVINGS

YEAST BATTER

¼ teaspoon active dry yeast or ½ teaspoon fresh yeast

¼ cup lukewarm (100° to 110°F) water

2½ cups all-purpose flour

A large pinch of salt, or more to taste

Approximately ¾ cup water

Olive oil for deep frying

3 medium zucchini, scrubbed and cut into ½-inch-thick rounds

In a small bowl, sprinkle the yeast over the warm water. Let stand until foamy, about 5 minutes. In a medium bowl, whisk together the flour and salt. Whisk in the yeast mixture, then gradually whisk in enough water to make a thick, smooth batter. Cover and let stand in a warm place until doubled in volume, about 1 hour. Preheat the oven to 200°F. Pour enough oil into a deep, heavy saucepan to come to a depth of 2 to 3 inches, and heat to 300°F over medium-high heat. (An electric deep fryer does the best job. Follow manufacturer's instructions for temperature.) Working in batches, dip the zucchini into the batter, letting the excess drip back into the bowl, add to the oil and fry until golden brown, about 3 minutes. With a slotted spoon, transfer the zucchini to a paper towel–lined baking sheet and keep warm in the oven while you fry the remaining fritters. Serve hot.

Olive Oil Note: Use any regular olive oil.

Fava Bean Fritters

Eating patterns are repeated all around the Mediterranean, and one of the oldest staples found in Western Europe, North Africa, and the Middle East is the fava bean. The fava bean sustained the peasants during the winter months and provided many tasty, nutritious meals. Today it is still an important ingredient in Puglia, where we have "fave e cicoria," and in Sicily, where "maccu" is still a favorite dish. It can be served as a nourishing broth or a pasta sauce. Leftover pasta and maccu is fried to make snacks, starters, and cocktail nibbles.

MAKES ABOUT 40

2 cups dried fava beans (10 ounces), rinsed and picked over

1 tablespoon olive oil

1 medium onion, chopped

1 ripe medium tomato, peeled, seeded, and chopped

1 tablespoon chopped fresh mint or fennel fronds

Freshly ground black pepper to taste

8 ounces spaghetti strands, broken into thirds

Salt to taste

1 cup all-purpose flour

Olive oil for deep frying

Place the beans in a large bowl and add enough boiling water to cover by at least 2 inches. Let stand at room temperature for at least 12 hours. (The beans can also be quick-soaked: Place them in a large saucepan, cover with 2 inches of cold water, and bring to a boil over high heat. Cook for 2 minutes, remove from the heat, cover, and let stand for 2 hours.) Drain the beans, and peel off the tough skins.

In a large saucepan, heat the 1 tablespoon oil over medium heat. Add the onion and tomato and cook until the onion is softened, about 5 minutes. Stir in the beans, mint, and pepper. Add enough boiling water to cover by at least 1 inch and bring to a simmer. Reduce the heat to low, cover, and cook, stirring often and adding more boiling water if necessary to keep the beans covered, until the beans are very tender, about 1½ hours. In a blender, in batches, or in a food processor, process the beans and their liquid to a thin, soup-like puree. Return to the pot and bring to a simmer over medium heat. Add the spaghetti and salt and cook, stirring often to avoid sticking, until the spaghetti is tender and the mixture is very thick, about 15 minutes. Spread evenly in a lightly oiled 12- by 8-inch baking dish, and cool completely. Cover with plastic wrap and refrigerate until firm, at least 8 hours.

Preheat the oven to 200°F. Cut the *maccu* into 1- by 1½-inch rectangles. Place the flour in a medium bowl. Dredge the bean pieces in the flour, shaking off the excess. Pour enough oil into a deep, heavy saucepan to come to a depth of 2 to 3 inches, and heat to 300° to 325°F over medium-high heat. (An electric deep fryer does the best job. Follow the manufacturer's instructions for temperature.) Working in batches, fry until golden brown, about 3 to 4 minutes on each side. With a slotted spoon, transfer to a paper towel–lined baking sheet and keep warm in the oven while you fry the remaining fritters. Serve hot.

Olive Oil Note: Use any regular olive oil.

Deep-Fried Spinach and Ricotta Pies

Pizzette, "little pizzas," do not have to be made from yeast dough. These deep-fried cheese-and-spinach-filled pies are made from a dough similar to that used for pastry. In fact, I have often used leftover pie dough, and it works very well.

MAKES 18

2 cups all-purpose flour

¼ teaspoon salt, plus salt to taste

2 tablespoons olive oil

1 tablespoon white wine vinegar

Approximately 1 scant cup water

¾ cup (6 ounces) whole-milk ricotta

1 pound spinach, stems removed, well rinsed to remove all traces of grit

2 tablespoons freshly grated Parmigiano-Reggiano cheese

1 egg yolk

Pinch of freshly grated nutmeg

Freshly ground black pepper to taste

Olive oil for deep frying

To make the pastry, mix the flour and ¼ teaspoon salt together in a medium bowl. Add the oil and vinegar, and using a fork, gradually stir in enough water to make a shaggy dough that holds together when pinched between your thumb and forefinger. Form into a ball, wrap in plastic wrap, and refrigerate for at least 30 minutes. To make the filling, place the ricotta in a sieve lined with cheesecloth set over a bowl and let stand for at least 2 hours to drain. Place the spinach in a medium saucepan, cover, and cook until the spinach is wilted and tender, about 5 minutes. (The water clinging to the leaves after rinsing is enough to cook the spinach.) Drain well and let cool. Squeeze the excess water out of the spinach and coarsely chop. In a medium bowl, combine the drained ricotta, the spinach, parmesan cheese, egg yolk, nutmeg, and salt and pepper to taste.

On a lightly floured surface, roll out the dough ⅛ inch thick. Using a 4-inch biscuit cutter, cut out rounds of pastry. Gather up the scraps, knead gently, and roll and cut out more rounds. You should have a total of 18 rounds. Place about 1 tablespoon of the filling in the center of one of the pastry rounds. Moisten the edges with water and fold over into a half-moon, pressing the edges together. Transfer to a baking sheet and press the edges with a fork to seal. Repeat with the remaining pastry rounds and filling. (The pizzettes can be assembled up to 4 hours in advance covered, and refrigerated.)

Preheat the oven to 200°F. Pour enough oil into a deep, heavy saucepan to come to a depth of 2 to 3 inches, and heat to 275° to 300°F over medium-high heat. (An electric deep fryer does the best job. Follow manufacturer's instructions for temperature.) Working in batches, fry the pizzettes, turning once, until golden brown, about 5 minutes. Using a slotted spoon, transfer to a paper towel–lined baking sheet and keep warm in the oven while you fry the remaining pizzettes. Serve hot.

Olive Oil Note: Use any regular olive oil.

Little Pizzas with Potatoes and Rosemary

Pizza is at its best when the topping is simple. Potato and rosemary is a popular Italian embellishment, unfortunately not well known outside of the Mediterranean. I make these as small pizzettes to serve with an *aperitivo* before the meal proper.

MAKES 12

1 large baking potato (about 8 ounces), scrubbed

1½ teaspoons active dry yeast or 1 tablespoon fresh yeast

¼ cup lukewarm (100° to 110°F) water

2½ cups all-purpose flour

Salt

3 tablespoons extra virgin olive oil

Approximately ¾ cup water

1 tablespoon chopped fresh rosemary

Freshly ground black pepper to taste

Cook the potato in boiling lightly salted water until just tender, about 20 minutes. Drain and let cool completely, then slice into ⅛-inch thick rounds. In a small bowl, sprinkle the yeast over the warm water. Let stand until foamy, about 5 minutes. Stir to dissolve the yeast. In a medium bowl, combine the flour and a large pinch of salt, or more to taste. Stir in the yeast mixture and 1 tablespoon of the oil, then stir in enough water to make a soft dough. Transfer to a floured work surface and knead until supple and elastic, about 10 minutes. Form into a ball and place in an oiled medium bowl, turning the dough to coat with oil.

Cover with plastic wrap and let stand in a warm place until almost doubled in volume, about 1½ hours.

Preheat the oven to 400°F. Punch down the dough. Turn out onto a lightly floured work surface and knead briefly. Pinch off 1½-inch pieces of dough and form into balls. You should have 12 balls. Cover with plastic wrap, and let stand for 10 minutes. On the floured work surface, roll out each ball of dough into a 4-inch circle. Transfer to lightly oiled baking sheets. Arrange the potato slices on top of the circles, and then brush the potatoes and dough with the remaining 2 tablespoons oil. Sprinkle with the rosemary and salt and pepper to taste. Bake until the crusts are golden brown, about 15 minutes. Serve hot. (The pizzettes can be baked up to 4 hours ahead and reheated before serving.)

Olive Oil Note: A full-flavored extra virgin olive oil will add the most flavor to the dough and the potato topping.

Italian Bread Baking and Salt

*T*he famous Tuscan bread, *pane Toscano*, is notorious in bread-baking circles for its lack of salt. One explanation for this omission is that when a particularly steep salt tax was imposed in the Middle Ages, the Tuscans chose to omit this expensive ingredient from their bread rather than be subjected to gouging. Actually, Tuscan cuisine has plenty of salt in its sauces, sausages, and stews, and the bland bread acts as a perfect foil to these full-flavored foods.

To the American palate, all Italian breads, Tuscan or not, may taste undersalted. Note that these yeast bread recipes only call for a large pinch of salt—a scant eighth teaspoon. Most American yeast bread recipes use about one and a half teaspoons of salt for every four cups of flour. Italians believe not only that a salty bread works against their highly seasoned food, but also that an excess of salt will retard the growth of the yeast and the dough's fermentation. (True, but only in very salty, practically unpalatable doughs, or when the salt is added to the yeast's proofing liquid.)

Please try these recipes in their authentic, reduced-salt versions. Then, if you find it necessary, you can increase the salt (the doughs will still work).

Olive Bread Ring

Freshly baked bread filled with black olives is a great treat. In the south of Italy, during lean times, this bread would often form the entire meal.

MAKES ONE 10-INCH ROUND BREAD

1½ teaspoons active dry yeast or 1 tablespoon fresh yeast

½ cup lukewarm (100° to 110°F) water

3¾ to 4 cups all-purpose flour

A large pinch of salt, or more to taste

3 tablespoons extra virgin olive oil

Approximately ⅔ cup water

¾ cup pitted small black Mediterranean olives, such as Gaeta

In a small bowl, sprinkle the yeast over the warm water. Let stand until foamy, about 5 minutes. Stir to dissolve the yeast. In a medium bowl, combine the flour and salt. Add the yeast mixture and oil, and stir in enough water to make a soft dough. Transfer to a floured work surface and knead until supple and elastic, about 10 minutes. Form into a ball and place in an oiled medium bowl, turning the dough to coat with oil. Cover with plastic wrap and let stand in a warm place until almost doubled in volume, about 1½ hours. If time allows, punch down the dough and let rise again for about 1 hour.

Preheat the oven to 450°F. Punch down the dough. Turn the dough out onto a floured work surface and pat and stretch into a thick, rough rectangle. Cover with plastic wrap and let rest for 10 minutes. Roll out the dough to a 20- by 8-inch rectangle. Sprinkle the olives over the dough and press them lightly into the dough. Starting at a long side, roll up the dough and pinch the seam closed. Transfer to a lightly oiled baking sheet. Form into a ring, bringing the ends together and pinching to seal. Cover with plastic and let stand until puffy, about 30 minutes. Bake until the crust is golden brown and the bottom sounds hollow when tapped, about 35 minutes. Cool completely on a wire cake rack.

 Olive Oil Note: Use a robust extra virgin olive oil.

Onion Focaccia

This can be offered as a first course or served throughout the meal as a savory bread. I often serve onion focaccia, along with a bowl of black olives and a plate of prosciutto, as a light lunch.

MAKES TWO 12- BY 7-INCH FOCACCIE

3 tablespoons extra virgin olive oil

1 medium onion, chopped

2½ teaspoons (1 package) active dry yeast or 1 tablespoon plus 2 teaspoons fresh yeast

½ cup lukewarm (100° to 110°F) water

4¼ to 4½ cups all-purpose flour

A large pinch of salt, or more to taste

Approximately 1 cup water

1 teaspoon dried oregano

In a medium skillet, heat 1 tablespoon of the oil over medium heat. Add the onions, cover, and cook, stirring occasionally, until the onions are softened but not browned, about 5 minutes. Transfer to a bowl and cool completely. In a small bowl, sprinkle the yeast over the warm water. Let stand until foamy, about 5 minutes. Stir to dissolve the yeast. In a medium bowl, combine 4 cups of the flour and the salt. Add the yeast mixture and 1 tablespoon of the oil, and stir enough water to make a soft dough. Transfer to a floured work surface and knead until supple and elastic, about 10 minutes. Form into a ball and place in an oiled medium bowl, turning the dough to coat with oil. Cover with plastic wrap and let stand in a warm place until almost doubled in volume, about 1½ hours.

Preheat the oven to 400°F. Punch down the dough and turn out onto the floured work surface. Gradually knead in the onions, which will give off their moisture and make the dough sticky. Knead in enough of the remaining flour to return the dough to its former texture. Form into two balls. Cover with plastic wrap and let rest for 10 minutes. Pat and stretch each ball out to an oval about 12 by 7 inches and about ¼ inch thick. Transfer the dough to lightly oiled baking sheets. Using your fingertips, make indentations all over the surface of the breads. Brush with the remaining 1 tablespoon oil and sprinkle with the oregano. Bake until the breads are golden brown and the bottoms sound hollow when tapped with a knuckle, about 20 minutes. Serve warm.

Olive Oil Note: A robust extra virgin olive oil will add the most flavor to the dough.

Potato Focaccia with Cherry Tomatoes

PUDDICA

In the days when the household's weekly supply of bread was baked once a week, potatoes were often added to the dough to prevent the bread from getting hard too quickly. This delicious speciality from Lecce belongs to the same tradition, and it makes an unusual starter served with fresh mozzarella cheese or prosciutto.

MAKES TWO 12- BY 7-INCH OVAL BREADS

2 small baking potatoes (6 ounces each)

2 teaspoons active dry yeast or 1 tablespoon plus 1 teaspoon fresh yeast

½ cup lukewarm (100° to 110°F) water

5 cups all-purpose flour, plus extra for kneading

A very large pinch of salt

¼ cup plus 1 tablespoon extra virgin olive oil

Approximately ¾ cup water

20 cherry tomatoes, halved lengthwise

6 garlic cloves, cut into 40 slivers

1 teaspoon dried oregano

Coarse (kosher) salt to taste

Cook the potatoes in boiling salted water until tender, about 25 minutes. Drain, peel, and mash. In a small bowl, sprinkle the yeast over the warm water. Let stand until foamy, about 5 minutes. Stir to dissolve the yeast. In a medium bowl, combine the flour, mashed potatoes, and salt. Add the yeast mixture and 1 tablespoon of the olive oil and stir in enough water to make a soft dough. Transfer to a floured work surface and knead, adding more flour as necessary, until supple and elastic, about 10 minutes. Form into a ball and place in an oiled medium bowl, turning the dough to coat with oil. Cover with plastic wrap and let stand in a warm place until almost doubled in volume, about 1½ hours.

Preheat the oven to 400°F. Punch down the dough and turn out onto the floured work surface. Form into two balls, cover with plastic wrap, and let rest for 10 minutes. Pat and stretch each ball out to an oval about 12 by 7 inches and about ½ inch thick. Transfer the dough to lightly oiled baking sheets. Using your fingertips, make 20 indentations all over the surface of each bread. Place a cherry tomato half and a garlic sliver in each indentation. Cover with plastic wrap and let rise until puffy, about 30 minutes. Drizzle the breads with the remaining ¼ cup oil, and sprinkle with the oregano and coarse salt. Bake until the breads are golden brown and the bottoms sound hollow when tapped with a knuckle, about 20 minutes. This bread is at its best served warm.

Olive Oil Note: A robust extra virgin olive oil will add the most flavor to the bread topping.

Pasta, Rice, and Soups

PASTA, RISO, E ZUPPE

In Italy these dishes are known as *primi piatti,* or first courses, which always surprises people who think they have already begun their meal with the antipasto. Of course, if you want to serve any of these dishes as a main course, it doesn't really matter where they are featured in the Italian menu. Years ago, when life was less prosperous in Italy, many families considered themselves very fortunate if they sat down to even one course, and for these lucky ones, pasta, rice, or soup was often the entire meal.

Tomato Sauce

⊛ SUGO DI POMODORO ⊛

August is the time to make fresh tomato sauce, when tomatoes are most flavorsome and abundant. Here's a recipe that should be in every cook's repertoire. It freezes beautifully (pack it in one- or two-cup containers), so you can enjoy it all year long. If you make tomato sauce in the cooler months, use canned tomatoes, preferably Italian plum, and hothouse basil. It is not worth using dried basil.

MAKES ABOUT 3 ½ CUPS

1 medium onion, chopped

2 garlic cloves, minced

2 tablespoons extra virgin olive oil

2 pounds ripe plum tomatoes, chopped, or 2 (28-ounce) cans peeled Italian plum tomatoes, drained, seeded, and chopped

½ cup packed fresh basil leaves, torn into small pieces

Salt and pepper to taste

In a large skillet, cook the onion and garlic in the oil over medium heat until translucent, about 5 minutes. Stir in the tomatoes and basil and bring to a simmer. Cook briskly, uncovered, until the tomato juices have evaporated and the sauce has thickened, about 15 minutes. If using fresh tomatoes, pass the sauce through a food mill (or press through a coarse strainer), discarding the peels and seeds. Tomato sauce made with canned tomatoes can be made smooth by pulsing in a food processor. Covered and refrigerated, the sauce will keep for 3 days.

Olive Oil Note: Use a good mellow extra virgin olive oil.

Summer Pasta Mediterranean Style

This dish is one of summer's great gastronomic pleasures, to be made only with the finest, most fragrant tomatoes. In fact, if the tomatoes are really sensational, you won't even need the Parmigiano-Reggiano cheese. The sauce has the added attraction of being uncooked, making for a cool summer kitchen.

MAKES 4 TO 6 SERVINGS

1 pound ripe plum tomatoes, seeded and cut into ½-inch cubes

8 ounces mozzarella cheese (preferably fresh), cut into ½-inch cubes, at room temperature

½ cup packed fresh basil leaves, torn into small pieces

¼ cup extra virgin olive oil

Salt and freshly ground black pepper to taste

1 pound penne or rigatoni

¼ cup freshly grated Parmigiano-Reggiano cheese (optional)

Toss the tomatoes, mozzarella, basil, and oil together in a large bowl, and season with salt and pepper. In a large pot of boiling lightly salted water, cook the pasta until just tender, about 9 minutes. Drain well, add to the tomato mixture, and sprinkle with the Parmesan cheese, if using. Toss well, and serve immediately.

Olive Oil Note: Use a good extra virgin olive oil.

Spaghetti with Artichokes

Some cooks make a creamy version of this dish, but I like this simple combination, which I prepare at least once a week during the spring artichoke season. If fresh mint is unavailable, you can omit it rather than substituting dried. Please use an excellent Parmigiano-Reggiano—an inferior cheese just won't do (although I have left out the cheese entirely and still had a wonderful meal).

MAKES 4 TO 6 SERVINGS

2 lemons, halved

6 medium artichokes (10 ounces each)

1 small onion, sliced

¼ cup extra virgin olive oil

Salt and freshly ground black pepper to taste

2 tablespoons boiling water

1 tablespoon chopped fresh mint

1 pound spaghetti

1 cup freshly grated Parmigiano-Reggiano cheese

Squeeze 1 of the lemons into a large bowl of cold water. Snap off the dark green leaves from 1 artichoke to reveal the light green center cone of tender leaves. Cut off the cone where it meets the thick base of the artichoke. Rub the cut surfaces of the artichoke with the remaining lemon as you work to prevent discoloring. Using a teaspoon, dig out the purple center leaves and scrape out the hairy choke. With a paring knife, pare away the thick green peel from the stem and base. Cut the artichoke bottom crosswise into ⅛-inch-thick slices and transfer to the lemon water. Repeat with the remaining artichokes. In a large skillet, cook the onion in the oil over medium heat until softened, about 3 minutes. Drain the artichokes, rinse well, and pat dry with paper towels. Add to the skillet and season with salt and pepper. Cook over low heat, stirring often, until the artichokes are slightly softened, about 4 minutes. Add the boiling water, cover, and cook over low heat until the artichokes are tender, about 10 minutes. Stir in the mint. Meanwhile, in a large pot of boiling lightly salted water, cook the spaghetti until just tender, about 8 minutes. Drain well, reserving about ½ cup of the cooking liquid, and place in a warm serving bowl. Add the artichoke mixture and cheese and toss well. If the pasta seems dry, add some of the reserved pasta cooking water and toss again. Season with plenty of pepper and serve immediately.

Olive Oil Note: Use an extra virgin olive oil. I like to use those from Puglia or Umbria.

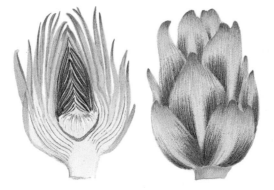

Spaghetti with the "Good Woman's" Olive and Tomato Sauce

There is a fine touch of irony in the name of this Neapolitan pasta. In the past, "good" women grew their own vegetables, or at least visited the local market every day to buy the best, freshest ingredients for their time-consuming dishes. Those slovenly women who spent their time in a more dubious manner had to rely on a quick sauce made from what was on hand in the store cupboard. Today we can all enjoy this easy, tasty dish, however we choose to spend our time.

MAKES 4 TO 6 SERVINGS

2 garlic cloves, minced

3 tablespoons extra virgin olive oil

1 cup black Mediterranean olives, pitted and coarsely chopped

1 cup green Mediterranean olives, pitted and coarsely chopped

⅓ cup capers, preferably packed in salt, well rinsed and patted dry

12 ounces ripe plum tomatoes, peeled, seeded, and coarsely chopped, or 1 (15-ounce) can peeled Italian plum tomatoes, undrained, and coarsely chopped

3 tablespoons chopped fresh flat-leaf parsley

Salt and freshly ground black pepper to taste

1 pound spaghetti

In a medium skillet, cook the garlic in the oil over medium-low heat just until it starts to color, about 1 minute. Add the olives, and cook, stirring often, for 2 minutes. Add the capers and cook for 1 minute. Stir in the tomatoes and parsley, bring to a simmer, and cook until the tomato juices have evaporated and the sauce has thickened, about 20 minutes. Season with salt and pepper (be judicious—the olives and capers can be very salty). Meanwhile, in a large pot of boiling lightly salted water, cook the spaghetti until just tender, about 8 minutes. Drain well and transfer to a warmed serving bowl. Add the sauce, toss well, and serve immediately.

Olive Oil Note: With this dish's assertive flavors, use an extra virgin olive oil.

Little Ears with Broccoli

This recipe is as versatile as it is delicious. I have called for broccoli, but traditionally Italian cooks make this with cauliflower or broccoli rabe. In Puglia, where the dish originated, turnip tops are used. The key is to cook whatever vegetable you choose until it is quite soft—no *al dente* vegetables here. Orecchiette (named for its ear shape) will trap the vegetables in hollows, but if you can't find it, substitute penne or fusilli. This is an everyday dish for everyday cooks, but the result is never mundane.

MAKES 4 TO 6 SERVINGS

1 large bunch broccoli (about 2 pounds), trimmed and coarsely chopped

1 pound orecchiette (or other pasta as suggested above)

6 garlic cloves, minced, or less to taste

¼ teaspoon crushed red pepper flakes

¼ cup plus 2 tablespoons extra virgin olive oil

Salt to taste

Bring a large pot of lightly salted water to a boil. Add the broccoli and cook until quite tender but still a nice bright green, about 10 minutes. Using a large slotted skimmer, transfer the broccoli to a colander and set aside. Add the pasta to the boiling water and cook until just tender, about 9 minutes. Just before the pasta is done, return the broccoli to the pot to reheat. Meanwhile, in a very large skillet, cook the garlic and hot pepper flakes in the oil over low heat until the garlic barely colors, about 2 minutes. Drain the pasta and broccoli well (give the colander a good shake, as water will be trapped in the orecchiette's hollows), and add to the skillet. Season with salt and toss well. Transfer to a heated serving bowl and serve immediately.

Olive Oil Note: Use any extra virgin olive oil.

Pasta Shells with Creamy Walnut-Ricotta Sauce

With its quick sauce that can be prepared while the pasta is cooking, this is a very good dish for the warm summer months, when the garden is full of basil. Fresh ricotta cheese, available at many Italian grocers, is always superior to the supermarket variety, so it is worth searching for.

MAKES 4 TO 6 SERVINGS

1 ½ cups (12 ounces) ricotta cheese, preferably fresh

⅓ cup packed fresh basil leaves, torn into small pieces

¼ cup extra virgin olive oil

Salt and freshly ground black pepper to taste

1 pound medium, shell-shaped pasta

1 cup finely chopped walnuts (4½ ounces)

In a medium bowl, stir together the ricotta, basil, oil, and salt and pepper. In a large pot of boiling lightly salted water, cook the pasta until just tender, about 10 minutes. Drain well. Transfer the pasta to a warmed serving bowl, add the sauce, and toss. Add the walnuts, toss again, and serve immediately.

Olive Oil Note: Use a delicate, mellow extra virgin olive oil from Liguria, Andria, or Bitonto.

Fettuccine with Walnut Sauce

This beautiful, flecked, pale beige sauce is best when served with the toothsome texture of ribbons of fettuccine or tagliatelle. In Liguria, the sauce is served with *pansotti*, ravioli-like pasta stuffed with wild herbs and cheese. Plain cheese ravioli are readily available here and are equally delicious with the sauce. To make the bread crumbs for this recipe, remove the crusts from day-old slices of coarse-grained Italian or French bread, and whirl them in a food processor or blender.

MAKES 4 TO 6 SERVINGS

⅓ cup coarse bread crumbs (from crustless stale bread, not dried bread crumbs)

¼ cup milk

1 garlic clove, peeled

1 cup walnuts (5 ounces)

½ cup freshly grated Parmigiano-Reggiano cheese

1 tablespoon butter

½ cup extra virgin olive oil

Salt and freshly ground black pepper to taste

1 pound fettuccine or cheese ravioli

In a small bowl, soak the bread crumbs in the milk for 5 minutes. Drain in a wire strainer, pressing against the bread to remove excess milk. With the machine running, drop the garlic through the feed tube into the bowl of a food processor fitted with the metal blade. Add the walnuts and pulse to finely chop. Add the Parmesan cheese and soaked bread crumbs and process until well combined. (You can also pound the garlic and cheese together in a mortar and pestle, and add the nuts, one or two at a time, pounding until smooth. Then stir in the soaked bread crumbs.) In the top part of a double boiler set over simmering water, melt the butter with the oil. Gradually stir in the walnut mixture and heat just until warm. Remove from the heat, season, and set aside.

Meanwhile, in a large pot of boiling lightly salted water, cook the pasta until just tender, about 3 minutes for fresh fettuccine, 8 minutes for dried, or 5 minutes for ravioli. (Test frequently to avoid overcooking.) Drain well, reserving about ½ cup of the cooking water. Transfer to the pasta to a warmed serving bowl. Stir enough of the pasta water into the walnut mixture to make a sauce with a creamy consistency, add the sauce to the pasta, and toss. Season with salt and pepper to taste. Serve immediately.

Olive Oil Note: Use a light, delicate extra virgin olive oil.

Spaghetti with Garlic and Olive Oil

Another quickly prepared pasta dish, this has sustained hungry Italians for centuries. It is a typical *cucina povera* recipe from Ischia, and one of my favorite places to enjoy it is at the trattoria Girasole in Sant'Angelo. One important warning: Do not allow the garlic to color too much or the dish will be unpleasantly bitter. A spicy variation is to add a dried hot chile pepper, torn into pieces, or crushed hot pepper flakes, to the garlic as it cooks in the oil.

MAKES 4 TO 6 SERVINGS

1 pound spaghetti

½ cup extra virgin olive oil

12 garlic cloves, coarsely chopped (not minced), or less to taste

1 tablespoon chopped fresh flat-leaf parsley

Salt to taste

In a large pot of boiling lightly salted water, cook the spaghetti until just tender, about 9 minutes. Meanwhile, in a medium skillet, heat the oil over medium-low heat. Add the garlic and cook, stirring often, until it begins to color, about 2 minutes; it should be very pale yellow, not golden brown. Immediately remove the pan from the heat, lift out the garlic with a slotted spoon, and discard it. Drain the pasta well and transfer to a warmed serving bowl. Add the garlic oil, parsley, and salt. Toss well, until every strand of the spaghetti is well coated with oil, and serve immediately.

Olive Oil Note: Use any good full-flavored extra virgin olive oil.

Pasta with Arugula

I love this simple pasta, and it is always the first one I make when I come home from my travels. It makes a marvelous quick snack when I am working late, invigorating me with its combination of tastes. In Italy, I use the strong-tasting wild arugula, but it is just as good with the cultivated variety found in the market.

MAKES 4 TO 6 SERVINGS

- 1 pound spaghetti
- 3 bunches arugula (about 1 pound), stems removed, well rinsed
- ¼ cup plus 2 tablespoons extra virgin olive oil
- 5 garlic cloves, minced, or less to taste
- 1 small dried hot red chile pepper, crumbled, or ¼ teaspoon crushed red pepper flakes
- Salt and freshly ground black pepper to taste

In a large pot of boiling lightly salted water, cook the pasta just until barely tender, about 8 minutes. During the last 30 seconds of cooking, stir the arugula into the water. Meanwhile, in a medium skillet, heat the oil over medium heat. Add the garlic and chile pepper and cook, stirring often, just until the garlic begins to color, about 1 minute. Remove from the heat. Drain the pasta and arugula well, and transfer to a heated serving bowl. Add the garlic oil, season with salt and pepper, and toss well, until the arugula is evenly distributed and each strand of pasta is coated with oil. Serve immediately.

Olive Oil Note: Use any extra virgin olive oil in this dish. I prefer those from Umbria or Puglia.

Deviled Spaghetti

This is a very unusual pasta recipe, in which the cooking water is heavily seasoned with garlic and chiles.

MAKES 4 TO 6 SERVINGS

6 garlic cloves

2 small dried hot red chile peppers

Salt to taste

1 pound spaghetti

3 tablespoons extra virgin olive oil

3 tablespoons chopped fresh flat-leaf parsley

3 tablespoons freshly grated Parmigiano-Reggiano cheese

In a blender, combine the garlic and chile peppers with 2 cups of water and process until finely ground. In a medium saucepan, bring 3 cups of water to a boil. Add the garlic mixture and return to a boil, then reduce the heat to low· and simmer for 15 minutes. Strain and reserve the spiced water. Meanwhile, in a large pot, bring 4 quarts of water to a boil. Add the spiced water and salt, and return to the boil. Add the spaghetti and cook until just tender, about 9 minutes. Drain well and transfer to a warmed serving bowl. Add the oil, parsley, and cheese and toss well. Serve immediately.

Olive Oil Note: Use a good-quality extra virgin olive oil.

Linguine with Lobster

A sumptuous special-occasion pasta found up and down the Italian coast. This particular version comes from Sardinia's fabled Costa Smeralda.

MAKES 4 TO 6 SERVINGS

Two 1½-pound live lobsters

3 tablespoons extra virgin olive oil

2 garlic cloves, minced

8 ripe plum tomatoes (about 1 pound), peeled, seeded, and finely chopped

½ cup chopped fresh flat-leaf parsley

1 pound linguine

Salt and freshly ground black pepper to taste

Bring a large pot of water to a furious boil over high heat and salt lightly. Add the lobster, cover, and cook for 3 to 4 minutes. Drain and let cool until easy to handle. Using a sharp heavy knife and a nutcracker, remove the meat from the lobster, reserving any juices, and cut the meat into ½-inch pieces. (The lobster will be only partially cooked.) In a large skillet, heat the oil over medium heat. Add the garlic and cook until barely colored, about 1 minute. Stir in the tomatoes and parsley. Bring to a simmer, reduce the heat to low, and cook for 10 minutes. Add the lobster and its juices. Cook for 3 minutes. Meanwhile, in a large pot of boiling lightly salted water, cook the linguine until barely tender, about 5 minutes. Drain well and transfer to a warmed serving bowl. Add the lobster sauce, season with pepper, and toss well. Serve at once.

Olive Oil Note: Use a delicate extra virgin olive oil, preferably from Liguria, Lake Garda, or Andria.

Pasta with Duck Sauce from Arezzo

Today it is quite unusual to see Italians eating pasta with meat sauce. Because pasta is served as a starter, and the main dish is usually meat or poultry, the sauce for the appetizer is usually light and based on fish or vegetables. In the past, however, when people ate more frugally, the juices from the meat dish would be used to dress pasta, and the meat served as a separate meal. This Tuscan duck dish would originally have been made with wild duck and certainly stretched to make two meals.

MAKES 4 TO 6 SERVINGS

½ cup extra virgin olive oil

One 4½-pound duck, cut into 8 pieces, rinsed, and patted dry with paper towels (liver reserved and chopped, if available)

1 medium onion, chopped

1 medium carrot, chopped

1 medium celery rib, chopped

4 ounces thickly sliced prosciutto, finely chopped

1 tablespoon chopped fresh flat-leaf parsley

2 bay leaves

1 cup dry white wine

2 pounds ripe plum tomatoes, peeled, seeded, and chopped, or 2 (15-ounce) cans peeled Italian plum tomatoes, drained and finely chopped

Salt and freshly ground black pepper to taste

1 pound pappardelle, fettuccine, or tagliatelle

½ cup freshly grated Parmesan cheese

In a large pot, heat the oil over medium-high heat. Add the duck and cook, turning occasionally, until browned on all sides, about 8 minutes. Add the onion, carrot, celery, prosciutto, parsley, and bay leaves. Add ¼ cup of the wine, bring to a simmer, and cook until it has evaporated. Add another ¼ cup wine and continue cooking, adding the wine ¼ cup at a time, until all of it has evaporated and the vegetables are softened, about 10 minutes. Stir in the tomatoes, season with salt and pepper, and bring to a simmer. Reduce the heat to low, cover, and simmer until the duck is tender, about 1½ hours. Add the liver, if using, during the last 10 minutes of cooking. Using a slotted spoon, lift out the duck and set it aside. (Keep the duck warm to serve on top of the pasta, or serve it as a second course.) Skim off the fat from the surface of the sauce. Transfer the sauce to a food processor and pulse until smooth, or press through a coarse wire strainer.

Meanwhile, in a large pot of boiling lightly salted water, cook the pasta until just tender, about 9 minutes. Drain well and transfer to a warm serving bowl. Add the warm duck sauce and the Parmesan cheese, toss well, and serve immediately.

Olive Oil Note: An extra virgin Tuscan olive oil would be excellent here.

Fisherman's Risotto

This is an extravagant dish when made with a bounty of various shellfish, but you can also prepare it with whatever is available in the market. A good broth (which this recipe provides) is the secret to a fine risotto.

MAKES 4 TO 6 SERVINGS

12 cups water

1 ½ pounds fish trimmings for stock, coarsely chopped

4 large ripe tomatoes, seeded and chopped

2 medium onions, chopped

1 medium carrot, chopped

1 medium celery rib, chopped

3 garlic cloves, 2 crushed and 1 minced

3 sprigs fresh flat-leaf parsley

Salt to taste

½ cup dry white wine

8 ounces cleaned squid, sacs cut into ½-inch-thick rings and tentacles chopped

1 pound large shrimp, peeled and deveined

1 ¼ cups extra virgin olive oil

12 mussels, well scrubbed and debearded

12 littleneck clams, well scrubbed

1 pound Italian short-grain rice, such as Arborio or carnaroli

Freshly ground black pepper to taste

2 tablespoons chopped fresh parsley

To make the fish base, in a large pot, bring the water to a boil. Add the fish trimmings, tomatoes, half the onions, the carrot, celery, 1 of the crushed garlic cloves, the parsley sprigs, and salt. Return to a boil, reduce the heat to low, and simmer for 25 minutes. Add the wine and cook for 5 minutes. Strain into another large pot, discarding the solids. Bring to a simmer, add the squid, and cook until the squid is just tender, about 1 minute. Using a slotted spoon, transfer the squid to a large bowl and cover with foil to keep warm. Add the shrimp to the stock and cook until pink and firm, about 3 minutes. Using a slotted spoon, transfer the shrimp to the bowl and cover. Bring the stock to a gentle simmer.

In a large saucepan, heat 1 tablespoon of the oil over medium-high heat. Add the clams, mussels, and the remaining crushed garlic clove. Cover and cook, stirring occasionally, until the clams and mussels have opened, about 5 minutes. Discard any that haven't opened, add the shellfish and cooking liquid to the bowl of squid, and cover to keep warm.

To make the risotto, heat the remaining 3 tablespoons of oil in a large heavy-bottomed saucepan over medium heat. Add the remaining onions and the minced garlic and cook until the onions are softened, about 5 minutes. Add the rice and cook, stirring often, until the rice has turned opaque, about 3 minutes. Ladle about 1 cup of the simmering fish stock into the rice. Cook, stirring constantly, until the stock has evaporated. Continue cooking and stirring, adding more stock only when the previous addition has evaporated, until the rice is almost tender, 20 minutes. It is important not to "drown" the rice in stock and to stir almost constantly. Keep any remaining stock at a gentle boil. Using a slotted spoon, add the squid, shrimp, and shellfish. Cook until the rice is *al dente*, about 5 more minutes. (If you run out of stock before the risotto is finished, you can use boiling water instead. You can add more stock or water to the risotto at the end to give the dish a loose consistency—it's a matter of personal taste.) Season with salt and pepper to taste. Transfer to individual serving bowls and sprinkle with the parsley. Serve immediately.

Olive Oil Note: Use a delicate extra virgin olive oil, preferably from Liguria or Lake Garda.

Light Stock

This is a basic stock with neutral flavor that can be used in many dishes. You can use either veal or chicken bones, or both. If I am making this stock for a particular recipe, I often add appropriate herbs during the last thirty minutes of simmering. For example, for Mushroom and Basil Soup (page 59), I add a handful of basil leaves so the finished stock will complement the flavors of the soup. This gives an added depth of flavor to the finished dish, but it is not imperative. Make this stock in large quantities and freeze it in one-pint containers for convenience.

MAKES ABOUT 1 1/2 QUARTS

1 pound lean veal shoulder with bones and/or chicken backs, chopped into large pieces

8 cups water

1 medium onion, chopped

2 small carrots, chopped

1 celery rib, chopped

6 black peppercorns

Herbs as desired (see above)

Salt and freshly ground black pepper to taste

In a large saucepan, combine the veal and/or chicken bones and water and bring to a simmer over medium heat, skimming off any foam that rises to the surface. Add the onion, carrot, celery, and peppercorns, reduce the heat to low, and simmer for 2 to 3 hours. During the last 30 minutes, add herbs as desired. Strain into a bowl, season with salt and pepper, and let cool to room temperature. Skim off any fat on the surface. The stock can be covered and refrigerated for up to 3 days or frozen for up to 3 months.

Mushroom and Basil Soup

⊱ ZUPPA DI PORCINI AL BASILICO ⊰

This lovely soup comes from beautiful Liguria, where the rugged mountains coming straight down to the sea leave little pastureland for grazing. Luckily, the mountain forests yield excellent porcini mushrooms (and the dramatic coastline has incomparable fish). Fresh porcini are a luxury in America, imported in small quantities during a very short season, but shiitake, cremini, and portobello mushrooms have a similar meaty texture and can be found in many supermarkets.

MAKES 8 SERVINGS

2 garlic cloves, peeled and halved

3 tablespoons extra virgin olive oil

1 ¼ pounds mushrooms such as shiitakes, with their stems removed, cremini, or portobellos, trimmed and sliced ¼ inch thick

6 cups Light Stock (page 58)

½ cup packed fresh basil leaves, torn into small pieces

1 large egg, well beaten

Salt and freshly ground black pepper to taste

In a large pot, cook the garlic in the oil over medium heat until light gold, about 2 minutes. Using a slotted spoon, lift out and discard the garlic. Add the mushrooms and cook, stirring, until lightly browned, about 10 minutes. Add the stock and basil and bring to a simmer. Reduce the heat to low and simmer for 5 minutes. Whisking constantly, slowly add the beaten egg in a continuous stream, and cook until the egg strands are firm, about 1 minute. Season with salt and pepper, and serve hot.

Olive Oil Note: A mellow, soft extra virgin olive oil from Liguria would be ideal.

Bean Soup from the Olive Mill

ZUPPA FRANTOIANA

I n Tuscany, the oil makers savor the very first pressings by making this robust soup. Similar soups are also to be found in Umbria. You can use any combination of bitter greens, but to be most authentic, you must include dark kale, which the Italians call *cavalo nero*. Big fat brown borlotti beans are the first choice, but cannellini or cranberry beans can be used instead.

MAKES 8 SERVINGS

3 cups dried borlotti or cranberry beans, rinsed and picked over for stones

1 large onion, chopped

2 celery ribs, chopped

3 medium carrots, chopped

Salt to taste

1 cup extra virgin olive oil, plus additional for serving

2 slices bacon, coarsely chopped

2 garlic cloves, 1 minced and 1 left whole

12 large kale leaves (about 5 ounces), well rinsed, stems removed, and cut into ½-inch-wide strips

3 cups mixed bitter greens (about 10 ounces), such as chicory, escarole, and/or radicchio, trimmed, well rinsed, and torn into 1-inch pieces

2 medium boiling potatoes (about 9 ounces), scrubbed and cut into ½-inch cubes

1 medium zucchini, scrubbed and cut into ½-inch cubes

1 teaspoon fennel seeds

Freshly ground black pepper to taste

Six ½-inch-thick slices coarse Italian or French bread

Place the beans in a large bowl, cover generously with cold water, and let soak overnight. Drain. Transfer the beans to a large pot and add enough water to cover by 2 inches. Add the onion, celery, and half the carrots and bring to a simmer. Reduce the heat to low and cook for 30 minutes. Season with salt and simmer until the beans are tender, about 30 more minutes. (The exact cooking time will depend on the age and dryness of the beans.) Drain, reserving the cooking liquid. Add enough water to the cooking liquid to make 4 cups. In a large pot, heat 1 tablespoon of the oil over medium heat. Add the bacon, the remaining carrots, and the minced garlic and cook until the carrots are softened, about 5 minutes. Stir in 2 cups of the reserved cooking liquid, the kale, mixed greens, potatoes, zucchini, and fennel seeds and bring to a simmer. Reduce the heat to low and cook until the potatoes are very tender, about 30 minutes.

Meanwhile, transfer the remaining 2 cups cooking liquid to a blender or food processor. Set aside 1 cup of the cooked beans, add the remaining beans to the cooking liquid in the blender, and process to make a smooth puree. Stir the puree and the reserved whole beans into the soup and simmer for 10 minutes longer. Season the soup with salt and plenty of pepper. While the soup is simmering, preheat the oven to 400°F. Place the bread on baking sheets and toast in the oven, turning once, until golden, 12 to 15 minutes. Rub the warm toasted bread with the whole garlic clove. Place half the toasted bread in a large soup tureen and drizzle with half the remaining oil. Pour in half of the soup. Lay the remaining bread on top of the soup, drizzle with the remaining oil, and pour in the rest of the soup. Serve hot, or let cool and serve at room temperature. (Thin the soup with water if it thickens upon standing.) In either case, serve with a peppermill for grinding and a bottle of extra virgin olive oil so your guests can add more oil as they wish.

Olive Oil Note: Use a young, robust extra virgin olive oil, from Umbria or Tuscany if possible.

Tomato and Bread Soup

This Tuscan specialty is superlative during the summer when plum tomatoes are bursting with flavor. It is usually served at room temperature (never cold from the refrigerator), garnished with a drizzle of excellent extra virgin olive oil.

MAKES 8 SERVINGS

12 ounces stale coarse Italian bread, cut into ½-inch-thick slices

2 pounds ripe plum tomatoes, chopped

5 cups Light Stock (page 58)

½ packed cup basil leaves, torn into small pieces

½ cup extra virgin olive oil

4 garlic cloves, minced

Salt and freshly ground black pepper to taste

Preheat the oven to 400°F. Place the bread on baking sheets and toast in the oven, turning once, until golden, 12 to 15 minutes. Tear into large pieces and set aside. In a large pot, cook the tomatoes over medium-low heat, covered, until they give off their juices, about 10 minutes. Pass the tomatoes through a food mill or a coarse sieve to remove the seeds and skin. Return the tomato puree to the pot and stir in the stock, basil, ¼ cup of the olive oil, and the garlic. Bring to a boil over high heat. Gradually stir in the bread pieces, reduce the heat to low, and simmer, stirring vigorously from time to time to break up the bread, until the soup is very thick, about 10 minutes. (If the soup seems too thick, thin to the desired consistency with more stock or water.) Season with salt and pepper. Serve hot or at room temperature, drizzling each serving with some of the remaining olive oil.

Olive Oil Note: Use a good extra virgin olive oil, preferably from Tuscany.

Chickpea and Pasta Soup, Pugliese Style

Lecce, in the heel of Italy, gives us this hearty, unusual pasta and bean soup dating back to pre-Roman times; the dish is virtually unknown outside of the Salento Peninsula. The combination of textures, with the firm chickpeas, soft-boiled pasta, and crispy fried pasta, is quite intriguing. I have given a soup version here, but if you prefer, you can make it into a pasta course by cooking the pasta separately in boiling water and tossing with the chickpea mixture for the sauce (this recipe will make enough "sauce" for about two pounds of pasta). Then garnish the whole with a handful of dried pasta that has been fried to golden-brown crispness in a few tablespoons of olive oil.

MAKES 8 TO 10 SERVINGS

1 pound dried chickpeas (garbanzo beans), rinsed and picked over for stones

Pinch of baking soda (optional)

1 bay leaf

Approximately 4 cups Light Stock (page 58)

1 medium onion, chopped

2 garlic cloves, minced

½ cup extra virgin olive oil

3 ripe medium tomatoes, peeled, seeded, and chopped

Salt and freshly ground black pepper to taste

8 ounces fettuccine

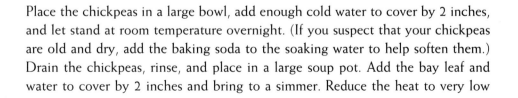

Place the chickpeas in a large bowl, add enough cold water to cover by 2 inches, and let stand at room temperature overnight. (If you suspect that your chickpeas are old and dry, add the baking soda to the soaking water to help soften them.) Drain the chickpeas, rinse, and place in a large soup pot. Add the bay leaf and water to cover by 2 inches and bring to a simmer. Reduce the heat to very low and cook until barely tender, 1 hour or more, depending on the age and dryness of the chickpeas (they can take up to 2 hours). Drain the chickpeas, reserving the cooking liquid. Add enough of the stock to the cooking liquid to make 10 cups. In a large pot, cook the onion and garlic in ¼ cup of the oil over medium heat until softened. Add the tomatoes and cook until the juices have evaporated, about 5 minutes. Stir in the chickpeas and the cooking liquid–stock mixture, and season with salt and pepper. Bring to a boil over high heat. Reduce the heat to medium to keep the broth at a gentle boil, add the pasta, and cook until tender, about 10 minutes. Season with salt and pepper.

With a slotted spoon, remove about 2 cups of the pasta and vegetables and drain well in a colander; keep the soup warm over low heat. In a large skillet, heat the remaining ¼ cup oil over high heat. Add the drained pasta mixture and cook, scraping the bottom of the skillet often with a metal spatula, until the mixture is crunchy and golden brown, about 10 minutes. Transfer the soup to a warmed soup tureen, top with the fried pasta mixture, and serve immediately.

Olive Oil Note: Use an extra virgin oil for the beans; you can use regular olive oil, rather than extra virgin, for the frying if you prefer.

Spicy Fish Soup from Maratea

ZUPPA DI PESCE ALLA MARATEA

Basilicata, the region between Calabria and Puglia, is still unknown to many travelers. It is a region of many contrasts, from the green meadows and mountain forests of Pollino to the limpid turquoise sea at Maratea, where this simple fish soup, substantial enough to serve as a main course, originated. Southern Italians make the soup with gray mullet. Here the more familiar porgy or sea bass is a good substitute.

MAKES 4 SERVINGS

3 pounds porgy or sea bass, cleaned

Salt and freshly ground black pepper to taste

3 garlic cloves, crushed

2 tablespoons extra virgin olive oil, plus more as needed

3 cups boiling water

½ cup chopped fresh flat-leaf parsley

¼ teaspoon crushed red pepper flakes

Six ½-inch-thick slices coarse Italian or French bread

With a large heavy knife, cut off the heads and tails from the fish and reserve. Cut the fish crosswise into 1-inch-thick steaks. Season with salt and pepper. In a large pot, cook the garlic in the oil over low heat until fragrant, about 1 minute. Remove the garlic. Increase the heat to medium. Working in batches, using more oil as needed, add the fish steaks and the reserved heads and tails to the pot, without crowding, and cook, turning once, until lightly browned on both sides, about 4 minutes. Return all the fish to the pot, and add the water, parsley, and red pepper flakes. Cover, reduce the heat to low, and simmer until the fish is very tender, about 30 minutes. (The consistency will be more like a stew than a soup.) Remove the heads (unless you like them), tails, and any large bones you can easily pluck out of the broth, and season the broth with salt and pepper.

Meanwhile, preheat the over to 400°F. Place the bread on baking sheets and toast in the oven, turning once, until golden, 12 to 15 minutes. Place a toasted bread slice in the bottom of each warm soup bowl. Use a slotted spoon to arrange the fish in the bowls, then ladle in the hot soup. Serve immediately.

Note: This soup is always cooked with the fish on the bone to give the fullest flavor. However, if served at a dinner party, the bones make refined dining a challenge. An alternative is to fillet the fish, reserving the heads, tails, and bones. Brown all the pieces with bones first in the oil, then wrap in cheesecloth and tie into a flat bundle. After browning the fillets, return the cheesecloth bundle to the pot, add the water, parsley, and red pepper flakes and simmer. Remove the cheesecloth bundle before serving.

Olive Oil Note: My choice here would be an extra virgin olive oil from the south.

Seafood

With Italy's long coastline, it is not surprising that food from the sea dominates the Italian table. In the past, the Church imposed various fast days when meat was not allowed, but I always feel that it would have been a much greater hardship to deny the Italians seafood. Since Roman times the sea's bounty has been greatly revered, and fish and shellfish are often served for the first three courses of a special celebration meal, although fish is often more expensive than meat. Away from the coast, the sale of fish is often confined to Tuesday and Friday, a relic of the Church fast days, but there is always a local trattoria ready to appease the craving on other days of the week. Italian cooks do not like to mask the flavor of fresh fish with complicated sauces, so here a good olive oil is indispensable.

Fish Roasted in an Olive Oil Bath

This is a simple recipe from the south, where olive oil, garlic, and parsley are often united to transform the humblest fish into something miraculously mouth-watering. Do not be miserly with the oil. Basting with this amount will keep the fish moist, as it should be, not crisp as in other roasted fish recipes.

MAKES 4 TO 6 SERVINGS

One 3-pound red snapper, sea bass, or grouper, cleaned, rinsed, and patted dry (see Note)

2 tablespoons chopped fresh flat-leaf parsley

3 garlic cloves, crushed

Salt and freshly ground black pepper to taste

1 cup extra virgin olive oil

Lemon wedges

Preheat the oven to 375°F. Lightly oil a baking dish large enough to hold the fish. Place the fish in the dish and rub inside and out with the garlic and the parsley, and salt and pepper. Pour the oil over the fish. Roast, basting occasionally with the oil, just until the thickest part of the fish appears opaque throughout when prodded with the tip of a knife, about 45 minutes. Transfer to a warmed serving platter. At the table, remove the head and tail. Using a long thin-bladed knife, remove the top two fillets. Lift off and discard the large central bone, revealing the two bottom fillets. Drizzle each serving with a spoonful of the cooking liquid, and serve immediately with lemon wedges.

Note: Two smaller fish, about 1½ to 2 pounds each, can be substituted. Roast for about 25 minutes.

Olive Oil Note: As this dish takes lots of olive oil, I use a blended extra virgin olive oil so that the cost isn't too extravagant.

Fish in "Mad Water"

Here's an old recipe from the time when Neapolitan fishermen used huge acetylene-fueled lights to attract the catch during nighttime fishing. These *lampare* gave off a great heat, allowing the ingenious fishermen to cook snacks on the flat, wide rims of the lamps. They would bring a cup of unpolluted Mediterranean salt water to a furious (mad) boil with olive oil, garlic, chile, and tomatoes, and add fish that had little market value to the cooking liquid. This modern version is equally simple and just as tasty. Be sure your tomatoes are very ripe, or else use the canned tomato substitution, but do not overdo the tomatoes—the sauce should be light orange, not bright red.

MAKES 4 SERVINGS

⅓ cup extra virgin olive oil

2 garlic cloves, crushed

1 small dried hot red chile pepper, crumbled

Two 1-pound striped bass or red snapper, cleaned, rinsed, and patted dry

2 ripe plum tomatoes, peeled, seeded, and chopped, or ½ cup canned peeled plum tomatoes

1 cup water

Salt to taste

2 tablespoons chopped fresh flat-leaf parsley

In a large skillet, heat the oil over medium heat. Add the garlic and chile pepper and cook until the garlic just colors, about 1 minute. With a slotted spoon, remove and discard the garlic. Add the fish and cook for 1 minute. Add the tomatoes and cook for 3 minutes, stirring the tomatoes around the fish. Pour in the water, season with salt and bring to a boil. Reduce the heat to low, cover, and simmer, basting occasionally with the cooking liquid, until the fish is just opaque throughout when prodded with a fork, about 15 minutes. Sprinkle with the parsley. Transfer the fish to a warmed serving platter. At the table, remove the head and tail. Using a long sharp thin-bladed knife, remove the top two fillets. Lift off and discard the large central bone, revealing the two bottom fillets. Drizzle each serving with a spoonful of the cooking liquid, and serve immediately.

Olive Oil Note: I would use a good, commercially produced extra virgin olive oil.

Baked Whole Fish with Black Olives

PESCE AL FORNO CON LE OLIVE

The sea dominates both Puglia's landscape, with its long, vulnerable coastline punctuated by ruined fortified farmhouses and Saracen towers, and its cuisine. Many traditional recipes are simple combinations of fresh seafood and southern Italian staples, like this marriage of fish and olives. It is very easy to prepare and cook, with a pleasing contrast between the firm olives and tender fish. Sea bream would be the first choice for this recipe in Italy. Here, use a very fresh grouper, snapper, or striped bass.

MAKES 4 SERVINGS

¼ cup extra virgin olive oil

One 2½-to 3-pound striped bass, red snapper, or grouper, cleaned, rinsed, and
  patted dry (see Note)

2 tablespoons white wine vinegar

Salt and freshly ground black pepper to taste

½ cup small Mediterranean black olives, such as Niçoise (unpitted)

Preheat the oven to 375°F. Pour 2 tablespoons of the oil into a roasting pan just
large enough to hold the fish. Place the fish on top and drizzle with the remaining
oil and the vinegar, then season with salt and pepper. Scatter the olives around
the fish. Bake until the fish is opaque throughout when prodded with a knife,
about 40 minutes. Transfer the fish to a warmed serving platter. At the table,
remove the head and tail. Using a long sharp thin-bladed knife, remove the top
two fillets. Lift off and discard the large central bone, revealing the two bottom
fillets. Serve immediately, spooning the olives and a little of the cooking juices
over the fish.

Note: You may also use two or three 1¼-pound porgies. Bake for
about 25 minutes.

Olive Oil Note: A good extra virgin olive oil is the best
bet here.

Drowned Trout Arezzo

Tuscan cuisine generally brings up images of robust soups and succulent meats, but there are many fish specialties too. Greatly prized are the trout of Arezzo, especially when "drowned" in this white wine and olive oil sauce.

MAKES 6 SERVINGS

4 trout (12 ounces each), cleaned

⅓ cup extra virgin olive oil

⅓ cup all-purpose flour

Salt and freshly ground black pepper to taste

½ cup chopped fresh flat-leaf parsley

2 garlic cloves, minced

1 cup dry white wine

Rinse the fish and let drain well, head down, for a few minutes. Pat dry with paper towels. In a very large skillet, heat the oil over medium heat. Dust the trout with flour, shaking off the excess. Add the fish to the skillet and cook, turning gently to avoid breaking up the fish, until lightly browned on both sides, about 5 minutes. (You may have to brown the fish in batches; return all the fish to skillet before proceeding.) Season with salt and pepper. Sprinkle the parsley and garlic around the fish and cook, stirring, until the garlic is fragrant, about 1 minute. Add the wine and bring to a simmer. Reduce the heat to low, cover, and simmer until the fish is opaque throughout when prodded with a knife, about 6 minutes. Using a slotted spatula, serve the fish directly from the pan, spooning some of the cooking liquid over each serving.

Olive Oil Note: Use a Tuscan olive oil if possible, but either virgin or extra virgin commercial olive oil is fine.

Baked Fish with Anchovy Crust al Gratin

In poorer parts of Italy, bread crumbs were often used as a substitute for un-affordable grating cheeses, giving a dish a browned crust that was called *gratin* even though the dish was cheeseless. Italian cooks would use hake (*nasello*) for this recipe, but any large white-fleshed fish will do. Make the bread crumbs by processing stale crusty Italian bread in a food processor or blender.

MAKES 6 SERVINGS

3 tablespoons extra virgin olive oil

¼ cup bread crumbs (from crusty stale bread, not dried bread crumbs)

3 tablespoons chopped fresh flat-leaf parsley

Salt and freshly ground black pepper to taste

One 3-pound red snapper, striped bass, or grouper, rinsed and patted dry

6 anchovy fillets packed in oil, drained and chopped

2 tablespoons fresh lemon juice

Preheat the oven to 400°F. Drizzle 1 tablespoon of the oil into a shallow baking dish large enough to hold the fish, and tilt to coat the pan with the oil. Sprinkle 3 tablespoons of the bread crumbs and 1 tablespoon of the parsley over the bottom of the dish and season with salt and pepper. Lay the fish on the seasoned crumbs, opening it up to expose the flesh. In a medium skillet, heat the remaining 2 tablespoons oil over medium heat. Add the anchovies and stir until the ancho-vies "melt" into the oil, about 1 minute. Drizzle the mixture over the fish. Sprinkle the remaining bread crumbs and parsley over the fish and season with salt and pepper. Bake until the crumbs are browned and the fish is opaque throughout when prodded with a knife, about 35 minutes. Sprinkle with the lemon juice to taste and serve immediately.

 Olive Oil Note: Use good, commercially produced extra virgin olive oil.

Soused Fish Fillets

SFOGI IN SAOR

*S*fogi in saor, sole fillets preserved in a spicy wine and vinegar marinade, is one of Venice's most famous and ancient dishes. It is particularly popular during the Feast of the Redeemer, which is celebrated with great rejoicing the third Sunday in July. The festival commemorates the passing of a great plague that decimated the city during the sixteenth century. The doge promised that if the plague abated, he would build a great church in thanks. When it did finally pass, the architect Palladio was commissioned to create the gorgeous Il Redentore on the tiny island of Giudecca, just across from Venice. During the festivities, fireworks light up the sky, and a special pontoon bridge of colorful boats connects the Giudecca with the Venetian seafront promenade, the Zattere.

MAKES 6 TO 8 SERVINGS

6 tablespoons olive oil, plus more as needed

2 pounds flounder or sole fillets, rinsed and patted dry

Salt and freshly ground pepper to taste

3 tablespoons all-purpose flour

2 medium onions, thinly sliced

1 cup dry white wine

1 cup white wine vinegar

¼ teaspoon ground cinnamon

⅛ teaspoon ground cloves

Salt and freshly ground black pepper to taste

⅓ cup golden raisins

2 tablespoons pine nuts, toasted in a dry skillet until lightly browned

In a large skillet, heat 3 tablespoons of the oil over medium-high heat. Working in batches, season the fish with salt and pepper. Dust the fillets with flour, shaking off the excess, add to the skillet, and cook, turning once, until golden brown, about 5 minutes. With a slotted spatula, transfer the fish to paper towels to drain. Add the remaining 3 tablespoons oil to the skillet, add the onions, and reduce the heat to medium-low. Cook until the onions are golden, about 10 minutes. Stir in the wine, vinegar, cinnamon, and cloves and bring to a boil. Cook until the liquid is reduced by half, about 5 minutes. Remove from the heat. In a medium glazed terra-cotta, enameled, or glass dish, arrange a single layer of fish fillets and season with salt and pepper. Cover with a little of the spiced liquid and scatter on a few of the pine nuts and raisins. Repeat the layering with the remaining fish, liquid, pine nuts, and raisins. Cover tightly with plastic wrap and refrigerate for at least 24 hours and up to 2 days. Remove from the refrigerator at least 1 hour before serving.

Olive Oil Note: Use a mild regular olive oil, as the heavy spices would cover up the flavor of a richer olive oil.

Baked Mackerel

In Italy, mackerel, bonito, sardines, and anchovies are known collectively as *pesce azzurro*, or "blue fish" (whereas on America's Eastern seaboard, bluefish is the name of a specific type of fish, which has the same blue-tinged flesh as its Italian relatives). All are regarded as everyday fish, costing much less than the more delicately flavored sea bass or bream. Here's just one ingenious recipe of many that make these commonplace fish more interesting.

MAKES 6 SERVINGS

2 pounds mackerel or bluefish fillets, rinsed, patted dry, and cut horizontally into 6 pieces

½ cup dry white wine

3 tablespoons extra virgin olive oil

1 large onion, sliced paper-thin

Salt and freshly ground black pepper to taste

3 tablespoons chopped fresh flat-leaf parsley

2 tablespoons fresh lemon juice

Place the fish fillets in a shallow glass dish and pour the wine over. Cover and marinate in the refrigerator for 2 to 3 hours. Preheat the oven to 350°F. Pour 1½ tablespoons of the oil into a large baking dish, and tilt the pan to coat the bottom. Spread the onion in the pan. Remove the mackerel from the wine and place in the dish. Drizzle with the remaining 1½ tablespoons oil. Bake until the fillets are just opaque in the center when prodded with a knife, about 15 minutes. Season with salt and pepper, sprinkle with the parsley and lemon juice, and serve immediately.

Olive Oil Note: Use any extra virgin olive oil.

Fish Baked in an Envelope

In Italy, I usually make this, one of my favorite dishes, with John Dory, which is called *pesce San Pietro* (St. Peter's fish) by the locals. This fish has two marks like thumbprints on either side, and legend has it that these were left by St. Peter's hands when he took pity on the fish he had caught and tossed it back into the sea. Substitute the more available sole or flounder.

MAKES 6 SERVINGS

6 sole or flounder fillets (about 7 ounces each)

¼ cup plus 2 tablespoons extra virgin olive oil, plus extra for brushing

3 tablespoons fresh lemon juice

2 tablespoons chopped fresh flat-leaf parsley

1 teaspoon fennel seeds

Salt and freshly ground black pepper to taste

Preheat the oven to 400°F. Cut six 16-inch square pieces of parchment paper and fold each in half. Cut each into a large, wide half-heart shape, as if making valentines. Unfold then brush lightly with olive oil. In a small bowl, combine the oil, lemon juice, parsley, and fennel. Season with salt and pepper. Unfold the parchment hearts and place a fish fillet on one half of each one. Spoon the oil mixture over the fish. Fold the other half of each heart over, and pleat the cut edges tightly to make a good seal. Place the packages on baking sheets and brush lightly with water. Bake until the packages are puffed and golden brown, 12 to 15 minutes. Place each package on a warmed dinner plate and serve immediately, allowing each person to slash the paper open with a sharp-pointed serrated knife.

Olive Oil Note: I prefer a mellow, extra virgin olive oil from Lake Garda or Andria, but you can use any good extra virgin olive oil.

Monkfish in Tomato Sauce

Monkfish is an evil-looking fish with a huge head. This recipe follows the traditional frugal Italian method of cooking an expensive ingredient in a sauce, reserving the bulk of the sauce to toss with pasta for another meal. You can follow their lead and serve some of the sauce with the monkfish, or serve all of the sauce and the fish with pasta for a more substantial dish.

MAKES 4 TO 6 SERVINGS

1 tablespoon extra virgin olive oil

2 garlic cloves, minced

5 cups Tomato Sauce (page 40)

1½ pounds monkfish fillet, cut into 1-inch cubes

2 tablespoons chopped fresh flat-leaf parsley

Salt and freshly ground black pepper to taste

1 pound linguine (optional)

In a large skillet, heat the oil over medium heat. Add the garlic and cook, stirring, until it barely colors, about 1 minute. Stir in the tomato sauce. Bring to a simmer, reduce the heat to low, and cook for 10 minutes. Stir in the monkfish and parsley, and season with salt and pepper. Cover and simmer until the fish is just opaque throughout when prodded with the tip of a knife, about 8 minutes. (If the sauce seems thin, lift out the fish with a slotted spoon, transfer to a plate, and cover with foil to keep warm. Increase the heat to high, and boil until the sauce has thickened nicely.) Meanwhile, if serving the linguine, cook it in a large pot of boiling salted water until just al dente, drain.

To serve, spoon 2 cups of the sauce over the fish, reserving the remaining sauce for another dish, or, combine all of the sauce with the linguine in a warmed serving bowl, toss well, and arrange the fish on top. Serve immediately.

Olive Oil Note: Use a good extra virgin olive oil.

Tuna "Pot Roast" in Tomato Sauce

❦ RAGÙ DI TONNO ❦

Sicily has a great many tuna recipes, including this one in which the fish is cooked in a tomato sauce.

MAKES 4 SERVINGS

10 fresh mint leaves

Salt and freshly ground black pepper to taste

2½ pounds tuna, in one piece

⅓ cup all-purpose flour

3 tablespoons extra virgin olive oil

1 medium onion, chopped

2 cups Tomato Sauce (page 40)

Sprinkle the mint leaves with salt and pepper. With a long thin knife, make ten 1-inch-deep incisions in the tuna. Force a mint leaf into each incision, pushing it below the surface of the tuna. Season the tuna with salt and pepper and roll in the flour. In a medium flameproof casserole just large enough to hold the tuna, heat 2 tablespoons of the oil over medium-high heat. Add the tuna and cook, turning occasionally, until browned on all sides, about 8 minutes. Transfer to a plate. Add the remaining 1 tablespoon of oil to the casserole and heat over medium heat. Add the onions and cook until softened, about 5 minutes. Return the tuna to the casserole and add the tomato sauce. Cover and cook until the tuna is opaque throughout and a meat thermometer inserted in the thickest part of the tuna reads 135°F, 35 to 45 minutes. If the sauce gets too thick as it cooks, add a little water. Cut the fish crosswise into thick slices and serve hot with the sauce.

Olive Oil Note: This robust dish needs a full-flavored extra virgin olive oil made from ripe olives, preferably an olive oil from southern Italy.

Raw Tuna with Lemon Juice

Although this is traditionally prepared with fresh anchovy fillets, tuna is an excellent substitute. (Of course, if you do find fresh anchovies and are up to filleting them, do so for an authentic treat.) This refreshing dish must be prepared with impeccably fresh fish. It makes an appetite-arousing first course, or it can be served with salad greens as a light summer lunch dish.

MAKES 4 TO 6 SERVINGS

1 pound center-cut tuna, in one piece, rinsed and patted dry

1 cup fresh lemon juice, plus more as necessary

1 cup extra virgin olive oil, plus more as necessary

3 fresh bay leaves, or 2 tablespoons chopped fresh flat-leaf parsley

3 tablespoons finely minced celery

Salt and freshly ground black pepper to taste

Wrap the tuna in plastic wrap and place in the freezer until very slightly frozen and firm, about 30 minutes. Using a thin sharp knife, cut crosswise into ⅛- to ¼-inch-thick slices. Arrange the fish slices in a single layer, without overlapping, in a large glazed-terracotta, enameled, or glass dish. (You may have to use two dishes.) In a medium bowl, whisk together the oil, lemon juice, bay leaves, celery, and salt and pepper. Pour over the fish, covering it completely. (The marinade must cover the fish completely so the lemon juice can "cook" the raw fish; stretch the mixture by adding equal proportions of additional lemon juice and vinegar.) Cover tightly with plastic wrap and refrigerate for at least 12, and up to 24, hours. Remove from the refrigerator 1 hour before serving.

Olive Oil Note: Extra virgin olive oil from Liguria would be the best choice, but any mild, mellow olive oil can be used.

Sicilian Swordfish with Potatoes

This swordfish specialty from Sicily, instead of being grilled, is cooked on top of the stove with tomatoes, capers, and olives.

MAKES 6 SERVINGS

2 tablespoons extra virgin olive oil

1 large onion, finely chopped

3 medium baking potatoes (about 1 ½ pounds), peeled and sliced ⅛ inch thick

6 ripe plum tomatoes, peeled, seeded, and chopped

2 celery ribs, chopped

½ cup pitted Sicilian green olives, coarsely chopped

2 tablespoons chopped fresh flat-leaf parsley

1 tablespoon capers, rinsed and patted dry

Salt and freshly ground black pepper to taste

6 swordfish steaks (about 7 ounces each) cut ½ inch thick

In a large nonstick skillet, heat the oil over medium heat. Add the onion and cook, stirring often, until softened, about 5 minutes. Layer half each of the potatoes, tomatoes, celery, olives, parsley, and capers in the pan, seasoning each layer with salt and pepper, then repeat the layering with the remaining ingredients (except the fish). Add 2 tablespoons of water, cover, reduce the heat to medium-low, and cook, shaking the pan occasionally to prevent scorching, until the potatoes are almost tender, 20 to 25 minutes. Add the swordfish, cover, and cook, shaking the pan every now and then, until the fish is opaque throughout when prodded with the tip of a knife and the potatoes are tender, about 8 minutes. Serve immediately.

Olive Oil Note: I recommend a Sicilian or Pugliese olive oil for this southern Italian dish, but you can use any mellow extra virgin olive oil.

Swordfish Marinated in Olive Oil and Citrus

Dried orange zest is the secret ingredient in many Sicilian dishes. It can be easily prepared by removing the zest (the colored part of the orange peel, not the bitter white pith) with a vegetable peeler and letting it dry until brittle in a warm spot—such as a turned-off gas oven with a pilot light—for about twenty-four hours. You can certainly substitute freshly grated orange zest, if you wish, but the authentic dried zest will become a welcome addition to your spice cabinet—try adding some to beef stews. The marinated grilled fish is sprinkled with fresh herbs, and you can use all five suggested, or just one or two.

MAKES 6 SERVINGS

¼ cup plus 2 tablespoons extra virgin olive oil

¼ cup plus 2 tablespoons fresh lemon juice

One 6-inch strip dried orange zest, crumbled, or freshly grated zest of 1 orange

6 swordfish steaks (about 6 ounces each), cut ½ inch thick (see Note)

Salt and freshly ground black pepper to taste

¼ cup finely chopped fresh tarragon, parsley, mint, oregano, and/or basil, in any combination

In a shallow glass dish, combine the oil, lemon juice, and orange zest. Add the swordfish, cover with plastic wrap, and refrigerate for 1 to 2 hours turning fish occasionally. Build a hot charcoal fire in a grill. Remove the fish from the marinade, draining well, and season with salt and pepper. Grill the fish, turning once, until barely opaque in the center, about 3 minutes on each side. Transfer to a warmed serving platter, sprinkle the herbs on top, and serve.

Note: Tuna, halibut, or cod steaks can be substituted for the swordfish.

Olive Oil Note: Use a good mellow extra virgin olive oil.

Grilled Swordfish Steaks with Mint Sauce

Although this recipe usually uses swordfish, other thick fish steaks can be prepared in the same way. Tuna, salmon, or halibut are all good. Mint provides a bracing, clean taste, making this a perfect warm-weather main dish.

MAKES 6 SERVINGS

½ cup chopped fresh mint

Grated zest of 1 lemon

¼ cup fresh lemon juice

¼ cup plus 2 extra tablespoons extra virgin olive oil

2 small garlic cloves, minced

Salt and freshly ground black pepper to taste

1 tablespoon chopped fresh flat-leaf parsley

6 swordfish steaks (about 7 ounces each), cut ½ inch thick

In a small bowl, combine the mint, lemon zest, 2 tablespoons of the lemon juice, 3 tablespoons of the olive oil, the garlic, and salt and pepper. Set aside. In a shallow glass dish, combine the remaining 3 tablespoons olive oil, 2 tablespoons lemon juice, and the parsley. Season with salt and pepper. Add the swordfish, cover with plastic wrap, and refrigerate for 1 to 2 hours, turning occasionally. Build a hot charcoal fire in a grill. Grill the fish, turning once, until barely opaque in the center, about 3 minutes on each side. Transfer to a warmed serving platter, pour the mint sauce over the fish, and serve.

Olive Oil Note: As most recipes for swordfish are from southern Italy, I would choose an extra virgin olive oil from Puglia.

Seafood Salad

❧ INSALATA DI MARE ❧

In summer, a cool serving of this vibrantly flavored salad makes the perfect first course or light luncheon. The octopus, squid, shrimp, and mussels and clams need to be prepared separately, but that job can be accelerated if you have a couple of pots going at the same time. I love dishes like this that can be made in advance so the cook can sit back and enjoy the meal along with the guests. Baby octopus is a popular Italian seafood. If you can't find any, increase the amounts of the other seafood to compensate.

MAKES 8 TO 10 SERVINGS

1 pound baby octopus, cleaned (see Note)

1 pound cleaned squid, cut crosswise into $\frac{1}{3}$-inch rings

1 pound medium shrimp

$\frac{2}{3}$ cup plus 1 tablespoon olive oil

2 pounds mussels, well scrubbed and debearded

2 pounds littleneck clams, well scrubbed

3 tablespoons fresh lemon juice

Salt and freshly ground black pepper to taste

6 large fresh basil leaves, torn into pieces

Cook the octopus in a medium saucepan of simmering lightly salted water until tender when pierced with a fork, about 45 minutes. Drain and let cool. Coarsely chop the octopus. In another medium saucepan of lightly salted water, cook the calamari until just tender, about 1 minute. Drain and let cool. Coarsely chop the squid tentacles. Cook the shrimp in a medium saucepan of boiling lightly salted water until they just turn pink, about 3 minutes. Drain, rinse under cold water, and drain again. Cut the octopus into ½-inch-thick slices. Peel the shrimp and devein if necessary.

In a large pot, heat 1 tablespoon of the oil over high heat. Add the mussels and clams, cover, and cook, shaking the pot often, until the mussels and clams open, about 5 minutes. Discard any unopened mussels or clams. Let cool and remove the meat from the shells. Place all the seafood in a shallow bowl. In a small bowl, whisk together the remaining ⅔ cup oil, the lemon juice, and salt and pepper until combined. Pour the dressing over the seafood, sprinkle with the basil, and toss well. Cover and refrigerate until cool. Serve chilled.

Note: You may substitute 1 pound bay scallops for the baby octopus. Cook in the lightly salted water just until opaque and firm, about 5 minutes. Drain, cool, and cut into ½-inch pieces.

Olive Oil Note: Use a light flavored extra virgin olive oil.

Deep-Fried Shrimp and Squid

Italians love their *fritti misti*, deep-fried mixtures of foods from fish, vegetables, and poultry to sweetbreads and brains. Deep-fried vegetables are usually served as a first course, while meats and fish are reserved for the main course. Here is one of the most favorite of all *fritti misti*, rings of tender calamari and morsels of whole shrimp.

MAKES 4 TO 6 SERVINGS

1 cup all-purpose flour

5 large eggs

Salt and freshly ground black pepper to taste

4 small squid, cleaned, sacs cut crosswise into ⅓-inch-thick rings, and tentacles left intact

8 ounces medium shrimp, peeled, leaving the tails intact, and deveined

Olive oil for deep frying

Lemon wedges

Place the flour in a large bowl. In a medium bowl, beat the eggs with salt and pepper to taste. In batches, dip the squid pieces and shrimp in the eggs and dip in the flour, shaking off the excess. Place on wire cake racks set on baking sheets and refrigerate for 1 hour to set the coating. Preheat the oven to 200°F. Pour enough oil into a deep, heavy saucepan to come to a depth of 2 to 3 inches, and heat to 350°F over medium-high heat. (An electric deep fryer does the best job. Follow manufacturer's instructions for temperature.) Working in batches, fry the squid and shrimp until golden brown, about 2 minutes. Using a slotted spoon, transfer to a paper towel–lined baking sheet and keep warm in the oven while you fry the remaining seafood. Serve immediately with lemon wedges.

Olive Oil Note: Use any olive oil suitable for deep frying.

Scallops, Venetian Style

Adriatic scallops are excellent, and the best recipes using them have a light touch so their natural flavor shines. Unfortunately, scallops are difficult to find in my Roman fish markets, so whenever I am in the Veneto, I like to order this. My favorite versions are those at Trattoria Nalin (near the villas designed by Palladio on the Brenta) and in any number of fish restaurants in Ravenna, the town famous for its mosaics. To enjoy this in a true northern Italian fashion, open up a bottle of Tocai.

MAKES 2 TO 4 SERVINGS

3 tablespoons extra virgin olive oil

2 garlic cloves, minced

1 pound bay scallops, patted dry with paper towels

2 tablespoons fresh lemon juice

3 tablespoons chopped fresh flat-leaf parsley

Salt and freshly ground black pepper to taste

In a large skillet, heat the oil over medium-high heat. Add the scallops for 2 minutes. Add the garlic and continue to cook, turning the scallops occasionally until just firm and opaque throughout, about 3 minutes. Stir in the lemon juice, parsley, and salt and pepper. Transfer to individual scallop shells or serving dishes and serve immediately.

Olive Oil Note: This delicate dish needs a light-flavored extra virgin olive oil. If it's available, choose one from Lake Garda.

Baked Mussel, Potato, and Rice Casserole

Every family in Puglia seems to have a different version of this casserole. Some add zucchini or other vegetables, others use potatoes only, and sometimes the mussels disappear altogether. The dish can be assembled in advance and refrigerated, then baked when ready to serve.

MAKES 4 TO 6 SERVINGS

2 pounds mussels, well scrubbed and debearded

2 garlic cloves, crushed

4 medium baking potatoes (about 1½ pounds), peeled and sliced into ⅛-inch-thick rounds

1 large onion, thinly sliced

2 tablespoons chopped fresh flat-leaf parsley

1¼ cups short-grain rice, preferably Arborio

3 ripe plum tomatoes, sliced into ⅓-inch-thick rounds

Salt and freshly ground black pepper to taste

¼ cup extra virgin olive oil

Preheat the oven to 375°F. In a large pot, combine the mussels, 2 cups of water, and the garlic and bring to a boil over high heat. Cover and cook just until the mussels have opened, about 5 minutes. Discard any mussels that fail to open. Remove the mussels from the shells, discarding the shells. Strain the cooking liquid through a cheesecloth-lined sieve into a small saucepan. In a large pot of boiling salted water, blanch the potatoes for 2 minutes. Drain well.

Lightly brush a 12- by 7-inch baking dish (preferably earthenware) with olive oil. Layer half the potatoes in the dish, then sprinkle with half the onions and half the parsley. Sprinkle the rice evenly on top. Spread the mussels over the rice, cover with the tomato slices, and season lightly with salt (be judicious, because the mussels may be salty) and pepper. Top with remaining onions and parsley, then the remaining potatoes, and season lightly with salt and pepper. Bring the reserved mussel liquid to a boil over high heat. Pour enough of the hot mussel liquid into the casserole to almost cover the top layer of potatoes; add boiling water, if needed. Drizzle the olive oil over the casserole, and bake until the potatoes are tender and the top is golden brown, about 45 minutes. Serve immediately.

Olive Oil Note: Use an extra virgin olive oil from Puglia if possible. If not, use any mellow extra virgin olive oil.

Mussels Baked in Their Shells

❧ COZZE GRATINATE ❧

On one of my first trips to Rome, a rather domineering waiter insisted that I try this dish. It was not something that I would have chosen, given the option, and I took up my fork rather resentfully. With the first taste, I forgave him everything, and have since made it one of my specialties. The mussels can be prepared up to four hours ahead, covered, and refrigerated, then baked when ready to serve.

MAKES 4 SERVINGS

2 pounds mussels, well scrubbed and debearded

¼ cup plus 2 tablespoons dried bread crumbs

2 tablespoons chopped fresh flat-leaf parsley

2 garlic cloves, finely chopped, or more to taste

Grated zest of 1 lemon

Salt and freshly ground black pepper to taste

3 tablespoons extra virgin olive oil

Lemon wedges

Preheat the oven to 450°F. In a large pot, combine the mussels and ½ cup of water, cover, and bring to a boil over high heat. Cook until the mussels open, about 5 minutes. Discard any mussels that do not open, and let cool. Remove the mussels from the shells, reserving half of the shells. Place 2 mussels in each reserved half-shell and arrange closely in a shallow baking dish. (If the mussels rock, line the dish with crumpled aluminum foil and nestle the mussels in the foil.) In a small bowl, combine the bread crumbs, parsley, garlic, lemon zest, and salt and pepper. Sprinkle the bread crumb mixture into the shells. Drizzle with the olive oil. Bake until the bread crumbs are browned, about 10 minutes. Serve immediately, with lemon wedges for squeezing.

Olive Oil Note: As the garlic and parsley flavors are quite assertive, use an extra virgin olive oil.

Stuffed Baked Squid

CALAMARI RIPIENI AL FORNO

There are an infinite number of recipes for stuffed calamari. This stuffing is simple but delicious. Some cooks also add chopped shrimp to enrich the mixture.

MAKES 4 TO 6 SERVINGS

6 medium cleaned squid, sacs about 6 inches long, tentacles finely chopped

½ cup dried bread crumbs

½ cup grated Pecorino Romano cheese

3 garlic cloves, minced

2 large eggs, beaten

1 tablespoon chopped fresh flat-leaf parsley

Salt and freshly ground black pepper to taste

2 tablespoons extra virgin olive oil

2 pounds baking potatoes, peeled and cut into very thin (less than ⅛-inch-thick) rounds

Lemon wedges

Preheat the oven to 375°F. In a medium bowl, combine the bread crumbs, cheese and garlic. Measure out ¼ cup of this mixture and set aside. Add the chopped squid tentacles, the eggs, and parsley to the mixture in the bowl, season with salt and pepper, and mix well. Stuff the squid pouches loosely with the bread crumb mixture (it will expand during cooking) and close with toothpicks.

Brush a medium baking dish with 1 tablespoon of the oil. Layer the potatoes in the dish, seasoning with salt and pepper as you layer them. Sprinkle with 2 tablespoons of water. Place the stuffed squid on top, sprinkle with the reserved bread crumb mixture, and drizzle with the remaining 1 tablespoon oil. Bake until the potatoes are tender, 50 minutes to 1 hour. Discard the toothpicks and serve immediately, with lemons for squeezing.

Olive Oil Note: Any good extra virgin olive oil is fine.

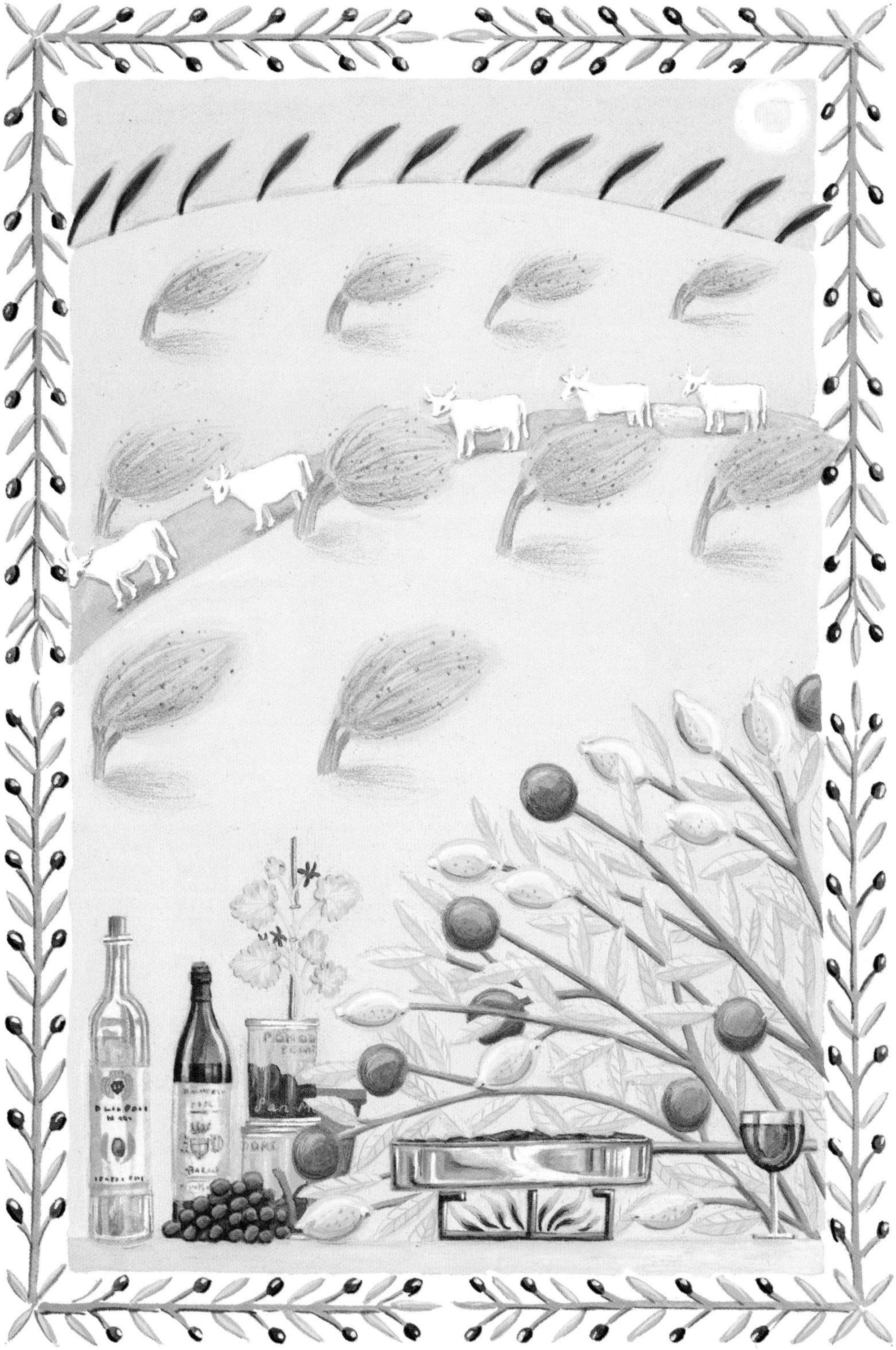

Meat and Poultry

Italy, like most Mediterranean countries, does not have the climate for lush pasturelands, except in Tuscany, where the famous white Chianina cattle, originally bred by the Etruscans and Romans for pagan sacrifices, are raised and highly prized. Elsewhere, animals are slaughtered when young to avoid having to provide them with costly feed during the winter months. Pork, dating from the times when every family kept a pig, and veal are the most common, but lamb and baby goat are served at holiday tables. There are many recipes for chicken since, again, most families kept chickens in their yards. Most Italian shoppers insist on seeing the meat sliced or chopped in front of them, viewing precut and prepackaged meat with deep mistrust.

Sliced Filet Mignon with Arugula

TAGLIATA DI FILLETO ALLA RUCOLA

Arugula, one of my favorite greens, is very fashionable on today's menus, found in antipasti, pasta, fish, and, in this case, beef dishes. It was a well-known herb in ancient Roman times, when it was considered an aphrodisiac and grown around statues of Priapus, the diety of lustful romance.

MAKES 6 SERVINGS

¼ cup extra virgin olive oil

8 ounces button mushrooms, trimmed, wiped clean with a damp cloth, and sliced

1 medium onion, finely chopped

Salt and freshly ground black pepper, to taste

2 cups dry white wine

6 beef fillet steaks (about 6 ounces each), cut 1 inch thick

3 bunches arugula, (about 1 pound), stems removed, well rinsed, and patted dry

Build a hot charcoal fire in a grill. In a medium skillet, heat the oil over medium heat. Add the mushrooms, onions, and salt and pepper and cook until the onions are softened, about 5 minutes. Add the wine and bring to a simmer. Reduce the heat to low and cook until the mushrooms are quite tender, about 10 minutes. Meanwhile, lightly oil the grill rack. Grill the steaks, turning once, until medium rare, about 8 minutes total. Transfer to a plate, season with salt and pepper, and let rest for 2 minutes. Slice the steaks. Divide the arugula leaves evenly among six dinner plates, place a sliced steak on each plate, and spoon the mushroom sauce over the meat. Serve immediately.

Olive Oil Note: Use a good extra virgin oil.

Florentine Beef and Chianti Stew

*S*tracotto literally means "overcooked," the procedure that gives this famous dish its complex, rich flavoring and melt-in-your-mouth texture. In the time of the Medicis, copious quantities of dried fruits, nuts, and spices were used to disguise the fact that the beef was not always at its freshest. Today, with quality ingredients, there is no need to add these embellishments. This recipe makes quite a bit of sensational tomato sauce, more than you probably need for the meat alone. Pour about two cups of the sauce over the sliced meat, and save the remainder to use in the best Italian tradition—tossed with pasta and served at another meal. For the best results, use a good Chianti for your *stracotto*.

MAKES 8 SERVINGS

One 3½-pound beef roast, such as top round or rump

3 garlic cloves, cut into 6 or 7 slivers each

¼ cup extra virgin olive oil

Salt and freshly ground black pepper to taste

1 medium onion, finely chopped

2 medium carrots, finely chopped

2 medium celery ribs, finely chopped

1 cup dry red wine, preferably Chianti

1 (28-ounce) can peeled Italian plum tomatoes, with their juices, coarsely chopped

Make incisions at regular intervals in the beef with the tip of a long sharp knife and insert the garlic slivers, pushing them beneath the surface of the meat. Brush with 2 tablespoons of the oil, and season with salt and pepper. Place on a plate, cover with plastic wrap, and refrigerate for at least 4 hours, or overnight.

continued

In a large flameproof casserole, heat the remaining 2 tablespoons oil over medium heat. Add the beef and brown on all sides, about 10 minutes. Transfer to a plate. Pour off all but 2 tablespoons fat from the pan. Add the onion, carrots, and celery, cover, and cook until the vegetables are softened, about 5 minutes. Add the wine and bring to a boil, scraping up the browned bits on the bottom of the casserole with a wooden spoon. Reduce the heat to low and simmer until the wine is slightly reduced, about 10 minutes. Stir in the tomatoes and their juices, and add the beef and any juices on the plate. Cover and simmer, turning the meat every 30 minutes, until it is very tender, about 2½ hours. Transfer the meat to a serving platter and cover with foil to keep warm. Spoon off any fat from the surface of the cooking liquid. Transfer the cooking liquid and vegetables to a blender or food processor and process to a smooth sauce. Return the sauce to the casserole and boil over high heat until reduced and thickened, 10 to 15 minutes. Season the sauce with salt and pepper. Cut the meat into thick slices and arrange on the platter. Ladle some or all of the sauce over the meat, and serve hot.

Olive Oil Note: If possible, use a robust Tuscan extra virgin olive oil.

Grilled Meatballs Wrapped in Leaves

POLPETTE IN FOGLIE

Barbecues acquire a Mediterranean flavor when small meatballs are wrapped in aromatic fresh leaves and grilled. West Coast cooks may have lemon trees and bay hedges at hand; be sure that the leaves have not been sprayed with toxic pesticide. Lacking fresh leaves, preserved grape leaves from a jar are an acceptable substitute. They will, however, change the flavor slightly. Or, if you are so lucky, use fresh grape leaves, softened in boiling water for one minute, drained, and rinsed. Choose young, tender leaves from the ends of the vines. While grape leaves are edible, lemon or bay leaves should be removed before serving. (Don't try to substitute dried bay leaves for fresh—they're too brittle and will break when pierced with a toothpick.)

MAKES 6 SERVINGS (ABOUT 34 MEATBALLS)

1 ¼ pounds beef ground round

½ cup fresh bread crumbs

½ cup freshly grated Parmigiano-Reggiano cheese

¼ cup chopped fresh basil or flat-leaf parsley

1 large egg, beaten

2 tablespoons water

Salt and freshly ground black pepper to taste

Approximately 3 tablespoons extra virgin olive oil

Fresh lemon or bay leaves or 1 (8-ounce) jar grape leaves, drained and rinsed

Soak a handful of wooden toothpicks in a bowl of cold water for 30 minutes. Drain well. In a food processor fitted with the metal blade, combine the ground beef, bread crumbs, cheese, basil, egg, water, and salt and pepper and process to a smooth paste. Using wet hands, form the mixture into thirty-four 1-inch balls. Brush the veined insides of the leaves with the oil. Wrap each meatball in 2 leaves (or just 1 grape leaf), oiled sides in, and fasten with the soaked toothpicks. (The meatballs can be prepared well ahead of time, covered, and refrigerated.) Build a hot charcoal fire in an outdoor grill. Lightly oil the grill rack. Grill the meatballs, turning occasionally, until cooked to your liking, about 6 minutes for medium-rare. Serve immediately, allowing your guests to remove and discard the toothpicks and leaves before eating the meatballs.

Olive Oil Note: Use any extra virgin olive oil.

Roast Veal Shank

Order whole veal shanks from the butcher to make this popular dish. The bones are very weighty, so each shank may weigh as much as four pounds. Tell the butcher *not* to saw the shanks into smaller pieces. Once you've acquired the proper cut of meat, the roasting is quite effortless. This is equally delicious made with pork shanks.

MAKES 4 SERVINGS

2 veal shanks (3 to 4 pounds each)

Salt and freshly ground black pepper to taste

2 tablespoons all-purpose flour

1 medium onion, chopped

1 medium carrot, chopped

1 small red bell pepper, cored, seeded, and chopped

½ cup dry red wine

¼ cup extra virgin olive oil

Preheat the oven to 375°F. Season the shanks with salt and pepper, then dust the veal shanks with the flour. Place the shanks in a roasting pan just large enough to hold them. Scatter the onion, carrot, and bell pepper around the shanks and pour in the wine and oil. Season well with salt and pepper. Roast for 1 hour, turn the meat, and roast until the meat is very tender, and a meat thermometer inserted into the thickest part of the meat, without touching the bone, reads about 180°F, about 2½ hours. (If the liquid threatens to simmer away, add water as needed.) Transfer the meat to a serving platter. Skim off the fat from the surface of the cooking liquid. Transfer the contents of the pan to a blender or food processor and process to a smooth sauce. Season with salt and pepper and pour into a large sauceboat. Carve the veal in thick slices parallel to the bone, and serve immediately with the sauce on the side.

Olive Oil Note: Use any good extra virgin olive oil.

Drunken Pork

⮞ MAIALE UBRIACO ⮜

To Italian cooks, Tuscany doesn't just conjure up visions of faded terra-cotta farmhouses and venerable cypress trees—it also means the country's finest meat. Butchers in other regions will often hang signs stating *carne Toscana* ("Tuscan meat") as an indication of quality. The Tuscan touch is evident in this superb pork recipe, with its use of Chianti and fennel seeds.

MAKES 6 SERVINGS

2 tablespoons extra virgin olive oil

6 center-cut pork chops, cut ¾ inch thick

Salt and freshly ground black pepper to taste

2 garlic cloves, chopped

2 tablespoons chopped fresh flat-leaf parsley

1 teaspoon fennel seeds

1 cup dry red wine, preferably Chianti

In a large skillet, heat the oil over medium-high heat. Season the pork chops with salt and pepper. Working in batches, brown the pork chops on both sides, about 6 minutes, and transfer to a plate. Add the garlic, parsley, and fennel to the pan and cook until the garlic barely colors, about 1 minute. Add the wine and bring to a simmer, stirring up the browned bits on the bottom of the skillet with a wooden spoon. Return the pork to the pan, reduce the heat to low, cover, and simmer until the meat is tender, about 45 minutes. Transfer the chops to a warmed platter and cover with foil to keep warm. Increase the heat to high and boil the cooking liquid until it has reduced to a thick sauce, about 5 minutes. Pour over the pork chops and serve immediately.

Olive Oil Note: Any good olive oil can be used, but an extra virgin Tuscan olive oil would be my first choice.

Pork with Red Wine and Juniper Berry Sauce

Wild boars used to roam the forests of Lazio, Umbria, and Tuscany, but they became such favorites on the Italian table that they almost became extinct. Now they are protected in special wildlife preserves, and the only "wild" boar available to cooks is raised on farms. Many cooks now substitute fresh pork in traditional boar recipes. Fresh pork leg is the best choice for this dish, but you can also use a bone-in pork loin. If you find a specialty butcher who will order wild boar for you, by all means try it. It will make a fine dish into something extraordinary, especially when served with polenta.

MAKES 10 TO 12 SERVINGS

1 bone-in leg of pork (fresh ham) (about 7½ pounds)

1 (750 ml) bottle dry red wine, preferably Chianti

4 garlic cloves, 2 crushed and 2 minced

15 juniper berries, crushed

2 sprigs rosemary or 2 teaspoons dried rosemary

A large sprig of fresh flat-leaf parsley

A large sprig of fresh tarragon or ½ teaspoon dried tarragon

A large sprig of fresh thyme or ½ teaspoon dried thyme

1 bay leaf

3 tablespoons extra virgin olive oil

Salt and freshly ground black pepper

Trim off and discard any rind or extraneous fat from the pork, leaving a thin layer of fat. In a large deep bowl, combine the red wine, crushed garlic, two thirds of the juniper berries, 1 rosemary sprig or 1 teaspoon dried rosemary, the parsley, tarragon, thyme, and bay leaf. Add the pork, cover, and refrigerate, turning the pork often, for at least 24 hours, and up to 2 days.

Remove the pork and pat dry with paper towels. Strain the marinade and set aside. In a large flameproof casserole, heat the oil over medium-high heat. Add the pork, season with salt and pepper, and cook, turning often, until browned on all sides, about 10 minutes. Add the chopped garlic and top remaining rosemary and juniper berries and cook for 1 minute. Add the strained marinade and bring to a simmer. Reduce the heat to low, cover, and simmer until a meat thermometer inserted in the thickest part of the ham reads 160°F, about 2 hours. (The pork can also be transferred to a preheated 325°F oven at this point and roasted for the same amount of time.) Transfer the pork to a serving platter. Spoon off any fat on the surface of the cooking liquid. Bring to a boil over high heat and cook until reduced to a thick sauce, about 5 minutes. Carve the pork into thick slices, arrange on the platter, and spoon the sauce over. Serve immediately.

Olive Oil Note: Use a full-flavored Tuscan extra virgin olive oil if possible.

Sausage with Grapes

SALSICCIA ALL' UVA

The Umbrian city of Norcia is renowned for its pork products, the sausages being particularly noteworthy. This specialty is best prepared in autumn, when grapes are ripe and plentiful and appetites crave more substantial fare after light summer meals. It is a very interesting combination of tastes and textures, well worth trying. In Italy, large, firm, plump grapes, not necessarily seedless, would be used. You may use a seedless grape variety, like Red Flame, but the seeded varieties are more authentic.

MAKES 6 TO 8 SERVINGS

2 tablespoons olive oil

2 pounds sweet Italian pork sausage links, pierced several times with a fork

6 cups seedless red grapes (about 2 pounds), without stems

In a large skillet, heat the oil over medium heat. Add the sausages and ½ cup of water and cook, turning occasionally, until the water has evaporated and the sausages are browned on all sides and cooked through, about 15 minutes. Transfer the sausages to a plate, and pour off all the fat from the skillet. Return the sausages to the pan, add the grapes, and cook over medium-high heat, stirring constantly with a wooden spoon, until the grapes are hot, about 5 minutes. (In a perfect world, the grapes absorb the cooking flavors without breaking, but I have never been completely successful with this part of the operation; even if some of them break, the taste is excellent.) Transfer to a heated serving platter and serve at once.

Olive Oil Note: Use a high-quality extra virgin olive oil.

Braised Lamb from Abruzzo

ᦉ **AGNELLO ALLA SCANNESE** ᦊ

The hilly Abruzzo region produces some of the best lamb in Italy. It is lean and tender, and since the animals graze on wild herbs, the meat has a great taste. But this simple recipe will make even supermarket lamb taste wonderful.

MAKES 4 SERVINGS

¼ extra virgin cup olive oil

2 pounds boneless lamb shoulder, well trimmed and cut into 1½-inch pieces (see Note)

Salt and freshly ground black pepper to taste

1 cup dry white wine, plus more as needed

3 garlic cloves, peeled

4 sprigs fresh rosemary or 2 teaspoons dried rosemary

Pour the oil into a medium flameproof casserole. Add the lamb and season with salt and pepper. Pour in the wine, add the garlic and rosemary, and bring to a simmer over very low heat. Cover and cook until the meat is tender, about 1½ hours. (Use a heat diffuser if necessary to ensure gentle simmering.) Check occasionally to be sure that the wine hasn't evaporated, and add more wine if needed. Using a slotted spoon, transfer the meat to a serving bowl and cover to keep warm. Skim off the fat from the surface of the cooking liquid. Bring to a boil over high heat and cook until reduced by half, about 10 minutes. Pour over the lamb and serve.

Note: Lamb shoulder makes fine stew, but it may be difficult to get your butcher to bone this particular cut of meat. You may substitute 3 pounds bone-in shoulder or neck, well trimmed, for 2 pounds boneless shoulder; ask the butcher to saw it into 1½-inch pieces. The bones will supply extra flavor and body to the sauce and add only a minimum of bother as you enjoy the stew. If you must, use boneless leg of lamb, but do not simmer longer than 45 minutes, or the meat may dry out.

 Olive Oil Note: Extra virgin olive oil is fine in this recipe.

Lamb Stew with Orange and Lemon

In southern Italy, local fruits are often used to give an extra dimension to meat dishes. In this stew, vinegar and sugar are added to make *agrodolce*, a sweet-and-sour sauce. The literal translation for this dish is "Lamb with Three Sours," being lemon, vinegar, and bitter oranges. Bitter oranges are hard to find in America, but some Latin American markets may have them seasonally. You may substitute regular orange juice or, to approximate the bitter orange flavor, a combination of orange, grapefruit, and lime juices in equal parts.

MAKES 4 TO 6 SERVINGS

2 tablespoons extra virgin olive oil, plus more as necessary

2 pounds boneless lamb shoulder, well trimmed and cut into 1½-inch pieces (see Note, page 103)

6 small white (boiling) onions, peeled

½ cup white wine vinegar

⅓ cup fresh orange juice, preferably from bitter oranges (see above)

⅓ cup fresh lemon juice

¼ cup sugar

Salt and freshly ground black pepper to taste

In a medium flameproof Dutch oven, heat the oil over medium heat. Working in batches, add the lamb, without crowding, and cook, stirring often, until browned on all sides, about 8 minutes; add more oil if needed. Transfer the lamb to a plate. Add the onions to the pot and cook until lightly browned, about 5 minutes. Return the lamb to the Dutch oven and add 2 tablespoons of water. Reduce the heat to low, cover, and cook until the lamb is tender, about 1½ hours. (Add more water, about 2 tablespoons at a time, as needed.) With a slotted spoon, transfer the lamb and onions to a plate. Skim off the fat from the surface of the cooking liquid. Add the vinegar, orange and lemon juices, and sugar and bring to a boil over medium heat, scraping up the browned bits on the bottom. Return the lamb and onions to the skillet and season with salt and pepper. Cook, uncovered, until the juices have reduced by half, about 10 minutes. Serve hot.

Olive Oil Note: Use a young, sharp extra virgin olive oil to complement the assertive flavors of the dish.

Green Lamb and Peas from Puglia

✦ VERDETTO ✦

The ancient Greeks were early residents of Puglia, and the Hellenic fondness for lamb has lasted through the years. In this dish, lamb and peas are simmered together for so long that the "green" that gives the dish its name becomes a rather pallid hue (*verdetto* is from *verde*, Italian for "green"). The Pugliese prefer their peas long-cooked in olive oil until they reach a yellowish color, making a tasty but visually unappetizing dish; I remedy this by adding some freshly cooked peas at the end of the cooking time for a colorful garnish. Whenever I cook peas, it reminds me of the time I served lightly cooked young green peas to an elderly lady from Lecce in Puglia. She looked at the peas and then plaintively asked her son what substance I had put in the pot to turn them such an unnaturally bright color!

MAKES 4 TO 6 SERVINGS

2 tablespoons olive oil

1 medium onion, chopped

2 pounds boneless lamb shoulder, well trimmed and cut into 1½-inch pieces (see Note, page 103)

Salt and freshly ground black pepper to taste

2 cups peas (2 pounds peas in the pod) *or* 10-ounce package frozen peas

2 tablespoons chopped fresh flat-leaf parsley

½ cup freshly grated Pecorino Romano cheese

2 large eggs

In a large flameproof casserole, heat the oil over medium-low heat. Add the onion, cover, and cook until softened but not browned, about 3 minutes. Add the lamb and season with salt and pepper. Increase the heat to medium, cover, and cook, stirring occasionally, until the meat is seared, about 15 minutes. Add 1½ cups of the peas, ¼ cup of water, and the parsley. Cover and cook until the meat is tender, about 1½ hours. (Check occasionally to be sure the water hasn't evaporated and add more water, 2 tablespoons at a time, as needed.) Meanwhile, in a medium saucepan of boiling salted water, cook the remaining ½ cup peas until just tender, about 3 minutes. Drain well, and set aside.

Using a slotted spoon, transfer the meat to a warmed serving bowl and cover to keep warm. Remove the casserole from the heat. In a small bowl, beat the cheese with the eggs. Gradually stir about 1 cup of the cooking liquid and peas into the egg mixture, and stir this mixture back into the casserole. Add the reserved peas. Return the pan to low heat and stir just until the sauce has thickened, about 1 minute. Do not overheat, or the eggs will curdle. Season with salt and pepper. Spoon the sauce over the lamb and serve immediately.

Olive Oil Note: I prefer a mellow extra virgin olive oil in this dish, although traditionally a Pugliese olive oil can be used.

Grilled Chicken with Fennel and Pork Stuffing

POLLO AL FINOCCHIO

With the assertive flavors of prosciutto, pancetta, and fennel, this chicken is very special indeed. I enjoy cooking this outdoors on a spit, but you can also cook it in a covered grill, as in the method described below.

MAKES 3 TO 4 SERVINGS

One 4-pound chicken, rinsed and patted dry

¼ cup extra virgin olive oil

1 tablespoon fennel seeds, ground in a spice or coffee grinder

4 ounces prosciutto, preferably imported Italian, cut into ¼-inch dice

4 ounces pancetta, cut into ¼-inch dice

4 garlic cloves, 3 minced and 1 left whole

3 bay leaves, ground in a spice or coffee grinder

Salt and freshly ground black pepper to taste

In a large bowl, combine 2 tablespoons of the olive oil and 1½ teaspoons of the fennel seeds. Add the chicken and rub the oil mixture all over the chicken. Cover and refrigerate, turning often, for at least 6 hours, or overnight.

In a medium bowl, combine the prosciutto, pancetta, minced garlic, the remaining 1½ teaspoons fennel seeds, the ground bay leaves, and salt and pepper. Loosen the chicken skin with your fingertips, then force some of this mixture under the skin. Put the rest of the mixture inside of the chicken. Rub the whole garlic clove over the chicken skin and brush with the marinade mixture. Build a hot charcoal or hardwood fire in one side of an outdoor grill. Place a baking pan on the other side of the grill, and add 1 cup of water to the pan. When the coals are covered with white ash, lightly oil the grill rack and place the chicken on the rack over the pan. Cover the grill and cook the chicken until golden brown and a meat thermometer inserted in the thickest part of the thigh not touching the bone reads 170°F, about 1½ hours. (Add more ignited coals after about 45 minutes, when the first fire has died down.) Let the chicken stand for 10 minutes, then carve. Serve a spoonful of the stuffing with each portion.

Note: If you have a spit attachment for your grill, use it by all means. The chicken will take about 1 hour to cook.

Olive Oil Note: I use Tuscan olive oil in this dish but it can be made with any extra virgin olive oil.

Chicken with Eggplant

The Arabs introduced the eggplant to Sicily during one of their many military forays into the area, but the locals, believing the vegetable to be poisonous, wouldn't touch it. During the Crusades, however, the Sicilian Carmelite monks noticed the eggplant being eaten with relish throughout the Holy Land. Upon their return home, they experimented by serving *melanzane* to beggars at the monastery gates, and when the beggars survived, eggplant found a place on the refectory table. Ever since, southern cooking has relied on this versatile vegetable.

MAKES 4 SERVINGS

4 small Italian eggplants (4 ounces each), trimmed and cut lengthwise into
½-inch-wide slices

1 tablespoon coarse (kosher) salt

¼ cup plus 2 tablespoons extra virgin olive oil

One 3½-pound chicken, rinsed, patted dry, and cut into 8 pieces

2 garlic cloves, chopped

1 cup dry white wine

1 cup peeled, seeded, and chopped ripe plum tomatoes (about 3 medium) or
drained and chopped canned peeled tomatoes

Salt and freshly ground black pepper to taste

1 tablespoon chopped fresh flat-leaf parsley

Place the eggplant in a colander and toss with the coarse salt. Set on a plate and let stand for 1 hour to purge the bitter juices. Rinse the eggplant well under cold water, drain well, and pat completely dry with paper towels. In a large skillet, heat ¼ cup of the oil over medium-high heat. Add the eggplant and cook, turning occasionally, until browned, about 5 minutes. Transfer to paper towels and set aside. In the same skillet, heat the remaining 2 tablespoons oil over medium heat. Add the chicken and cook, turning often, until browned on all sides, about 10 minutes. Add the garlic and cook until it just colors, about 1 minute. Add the wine, bring to a boil, and cook until most of it has evaporated. Stir in the tomatoes and season with salt and pepper. Reduce the heat to low, cover, and simmer until the chicken shows no sign of pink at the bone when pierced with a knife, about 35 minutes. During the last 10 minutes of cooking, stir in the reserved eggplant. Sprinkle with the parsley and serve immediately.

Olive Oil Note: Use any good extra virgin olive oil.

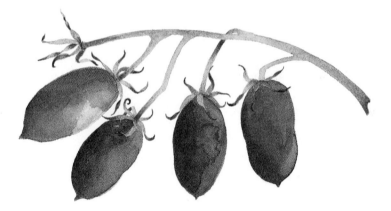

Warm Cornish Hen Salad with Balsamic Vinegar Dressing

My poultry market supplies me with gorgeous guinea fowl for this dish, but it will work just as well with Cornish game hens or their relatives, poussins. An excellent balsamic vinegar is what gives this dish its true character. Supermarket balsamic vinegars, commercially produced in bulk, are poor imitations of the traditional, artisanal vinegars from Modena made in small quantities by a slow and costly process originating around the days of Lucrezia Borgia. True balsamico can cost a duke's ransom, having to pass stringent taste tests by a consortium before being put up in distinctive squat bottles. Look for the best balsamic vinegar you can afford at specialty food stores, as, in this case, price is usually an indication of quality. (When my house was burgled last year, the thieves were obviously gentlemen of discernment, as their booty included a bottle of my best balsamico.)

MAKES 4 SERVINGS

2 Cornish game hens (about 1 ½ pounds each), rinsed and patted dry

Salt and freshly ground black pepper to taste

½ cup plus 1 tablespoon extra virgin olive oil

4 garlic cloves, peeled

3 small sprigs fresh rosemary or 1 teaspoon dried rosemary

3 sprigs fresh thyme or ½ teaspoon dried thyme

1 cup dry white wine

1 tablespoon plus 1 teaspoon balsamic vinegar, divided

6 cups mixed salad greens, such as arugula, radicchio, red oak, and/or
    Bibb lettuces

2 tablespoons pine nuts

Using a cleaver or large heavy knife, cut through the ribs down one side of the backbone of 1 of the game hens, cut down the other side and remove the backbone. Open out like a book and place the hen breast-side up. Flatten by pushing down very heavily on the breast. Season on both sides with salt and pepper. Repeat with the other hen. In a very large heavy skillet, heat ¼ cup of the oil over medium heat. (If necessary, use 2 skillets, dividing the oil evenly between them.) Place the hens skin side down in the skillet and add the garlic, rosemary, and thyme. Cover and cook, turning occasionally, until the juices run clear yellow with no sign of pink when a thigh is pierced with a knife, about 45 minutes. As the hens cook, add about 2 tablespoons of wine to the skillet every 10 minutes, using ½ cup of the wine in all. Remove the hens from the skillet and split each one in half, removing the breast bones if desired. Cover and keep warm.

Strain the cooking juices into a heatproof bowl and skim any fat from the surface. Return the juices to the skillet, add the remaining ½ cup wine and bring to a boil over high heat. Boil until reduced by half. Meanwhile, in a small bowl, whisk together the remaining ¼ cup plus 1 tablespoon oil, 1 tablespoon of the vinegar, and salt and pepper to taste. In a large bowl, toss the salad greens with the dressing. Divide the salad among four large plates, and place the Cornish hens on top. Scatter the pine nuts over, drizzle with the reduced pan juices, and sprinkle with the remaining 1 teaspoon vinegar. Serve immediately.

Olive Oil Note: Any good extra virgin olive oil can be used for the cooking. For the dressing, use a mellow extra virgin olive oil.

Tuscan Fried Chicken and Artichokes

POLLO E CARCIOFI, FRITTI ALLA TOSCANA

Renaissance court banquets were elaborate affairs, enjoyed equally by princes, courtiers, and artists. The long tables were adorned with great slabs of meat laden with herbs, dried fruits, and nuts and roasted to golden perfection. Vegetables were "gilded," too, by being deep-fried until golden brown. In this recipe, both the chicken and the artichokes get the "gold-dipped" treatment. Catherine de Médicis had a passion for artichokes, establishing enormous gardens of the vegetable at her French estate, and almost dying of an artichoke overdose late in life. Italians use baby artichokes in this recipe, so if you find them, use them—don't worry about digging out the choke, and cut them lengthwise in half, not into quarters.

MAKES 4 SERVINGS

2 tablespoons red wine vinegar or cider vinegar

6 medium artichokes (about 8 ounces each)

1 cup all-purpose flour

3 large eggs

Salt and freshly ground black pepper to taste

1 pound boneless, skinless chicken thighs, cut into 12 pieces

Olive oil for deep frying

Stir the vinegar into a large bowl of cold water. With a paring knife, pare away the thick green peel from the stem and base of 1 of the artichokes. Snap off the dark green outer leaves to reveal the light green center cone. Cut off the cone where it meets the thick base. Using the tip of a spoon, dig out the purple leaves and hairy choke from the center. Cut the artichoke into quarters, and place in the vinegar-water. Repeat with the remaining artichokes. Place the flour in a large shallow bowl. In a medium bowl, beat the eggs with salt and pepper to taste.

Drain the artichokes and pat dry with paper towels. Working in batches, roll the chicken and artichoke pieces in the flour, shaking off the excess and dip in the beaten eggs. Place on wire cake racks on a baking sheet and refrigerate for 1 hour to set the coating.

Preheat the oven to 200°F. Pour enough oil into a deep, heavy saucepan to come to a depth of 2 to 3 inches, and heat to 350°F over medium-high heat. (An electric deep fryer does the best job. Follow manufacturer's instructions for temperature.) In batches, fry artichokes first, and then the chicken until golden brown, about 6 minutes. Using a slotted spoon, transfer to a paper towel–lined baking sheet, and keep warm in the oven while you fry the remaining batches. Serve immediately.

Olive Oil Note: Use an olive oil suitable for deep frying.

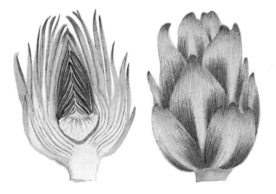

Chicken in Herb Sauce

Fragrant lemon zest and a profusion of fresh herbs give a particularly Mediterranean flavor to this easy chicken fricassee, which creates a creamy sauce perfect for spooning over rice. Fresh parsley and mint are essential for this dish, even if you must use the dried version of the other herbs.

MAKES 6 SERVINGS

¼ cup extra virgin olive oil

6 chicken leg-thigh quarters (drumsticks with thighs attached) (about 4½ pounds)

Salt and freshly ground black pepper to taste

1 medium onion, chopped

2 tablespoons all-purpose flour

2 cups hot chicken stock, preferably homemade

1 cup chopped fresh flat-leaf parsley

⅓ cup chopped fresh mint

3 garlic cloves, minced

½ cup chopped fresh chives

Sprig of fresh rosemary or 1 teaspoon dried rosemary

2 bay leaves

1 cup milk

Grated zest of 2 lemons

In a large skillet, heat the oil over medium heat. Season the chicken with salt and pepper, add to the skillet, and cook, turning often, until lightly browned on all sides, about 6 minutes. Pour off all but 2 tablespoons of the fat from the pan. Add the onion and cook until softened, about 3 minutes. Sprinkle the flour over the onions and stir well so that it blends with the pan juices, then gradually stir in the hot stock. Cover, reduce the heat to low, and cook for 30 minutes. Sprinkle the parsley, mint, garlic, ¼ cup of the fresh chives, the rosemary, and bay leaves over the chicken and stir in the milk and lemon zest. Bring to a simmer and cook, uncovered, until the sauce has thickened slightly and the chicken shows no sign of pink at the bone when pierced with a knife, about 15 minutes longer. Transfer the chicken to a deep serving bowl and cover with foil to keep warm. Skim off any fat from the sauce, bring to a boil, and cook until thickened, about 10 minutes. Remove the rosemary sprig, if using, and bay leaves from the sauce, season with salt and pepper, and pour over the chicken. Sprinkle with the remaining ¼ cup chives and serve immediately.

Olive Oil Note: Use a light-flavored extra virgin olive oil so as not to overwhelm the delicate herbs in the sauce.

Chicken with White Beans

Both the chicken stew and the beans can be prepared in advance and reheated, making this an ideal dish for the end of a busy day. The recipe is easily doubled if you want to make it for a crowd. Many bean recipes tend to be heavy, so it is interesting to see how the lemon slices and rosé wine "lighten" the dish.

MAKES 6 SERVINGS

1½ cups dried cannellini (white kidney) beans (12 ounces), rinsed and picked over

Sprig of fresh thyme or ¼ teaspoon dried thyme

Small sprig of fresh rosemary or ½ teaspoon dried rosemary

3 bay leaves

1 cup rosé wine

¼ cup white wine vinegar

6 small white (boiling) onions, peeled

2 small leeks, thinly sliced and well rinsed

3 lemon slices, seeds removed

2 whole cloves

6 chicken leg-thigh quarters (drumsticks with thighs attached) (about 4½ pounds)

Salt and freshly ground black pepper to taste

2 tablespoons extra virgin olive oil

Place the beans in a large bowl, add enough cold water to cover by 2 inches, and let stand at room temperature overnight. Drain the beans and place in a large saucepan. Add the thyme, rosemary, 1 of the bay leaves, and enough cold water to cover by 2 inches. Bring to a simmer over medium heat. Reduce the heat to low, cover, and simmer for 20 minutes. Season with salt and continue cooking until the beans are just tender, about 20 minutes longer. (The exact cooking time will depend on the age and dryness of the beans.) Remove the herb sprigs, if using, season the beans with pepper, and keep warm over very low heat.

Meanwhile, season the chicken with salt and pepper. In a large casserole, combine the wine, vinegar, onions, leeks, lemon slices, cloves, and the remaining 2 bay leaves, then add the chicken. Bring to a simmer over medium heat. Partially cover the pan and simmer until the chicken shows no sign of pink at the bone when pierced with a sharp knife, about 35 minutes. Drain the beans, place in a large warmed serving bowl, and toss with the oil. Arrange the chicken on the beans and spoon the sauce over. Serve immediately.

Olive Oil Note: I use a fruity extra virgin olive oil from the Abruzzo called Montinor, but any mellow extra virgin olive oil can be used.

Chicken Breasts with Shallots and Cherry Tomatoes

Here's a tasty entrée that shows how a simple marinade can add elegance to an uncomplicated dish. In Italy, I make this with breasts of guinea fowl, but chicken breasts (preferably free-range) will give similar results. A word about shallots: Often, upon peeling one, you find that the single shallot is actually formed from two cloves. Pull the shallot apart into two separate cloves, as the large, unseparated shallot may be too big to cook through.

MAKES 6 SERVINGS

1 cup dry white wine

⅓ cup extra virgin olive oil

6 medium shallots, peeled (1 chopped and 5 left whole)

6 chicken breasts (about 12 ounces each)

Salt and freshly ground black pepper to taste

1 pound ripe cherry tomatoes

3 sprigs fresh rosemary or 1 teaspoon dried rosemary

1 tablespoon chopped fresh flat-leaf parsley

In a large bowl, combine the wine, olive oil, and 1 chopped shallot. Season the chicken with salt and pepper and add to the wine mixture. Turn the chicken to coat, then marinate for at least 1 hour, turning the chicken from time to time.

(If marinating for longer than an hour, cover and refrigerate.) Transfer the chicken to a plate. Strain the marinade into a large skillet and add the remaining shallots cut into segments. Bring to a simmer over medium-low heat and simmer for 3 minutes. Add the chicken, tomatoes, and rosemary, cover, and simmer until the chicken shows no sign of pink at the bone when pierced with a sharp knife, about 30 minutes. Transfer to a serving platter and cover with foil to keep warm. Increase the heat to high and boil the sauce, uncovered, until it has reduced by half, about 5 minutes. Remove the rosemary sprig, if using, and season with salt and pepper. Pour over the chicken, sprinkle with the parsley, and serve immediately.

Olive Oil Note: My favorite olive oil for this dish comes from Spoleto in Umbria, but any good extra virgin olive oil is fine.

Vegetables

Vegetables play a very important part in the Italian way of life, so important that they are usually ordered and served separately in restaurants as *contorni*, or side dishes. Even at home, they are presented on a separate plate, and they are not seen as a mere accompaniment to fish or meat. Today, when for most people the vegetable garden is not even a distant memory, fresh vegetables and salads are still seen as a daily necessity, and street markets do a brisk trade keeping urban families happy.

Green Vegetables
with Lemon and Olive Oil

Trattorias all over Italy serve this as a room-temperature side dish, but it can also be enjoyed as a salad. Many vegetables are prepared in this simple manner—escarole, broccoli, and spinach are just a few. Here I give instructions for green beans. Cook them in advance and let them cool, but don't dress them until just before serving, or the lemon juice will turn their bright green color an unappetizing drab olive gray. In Italy, the very thin and delicate green beans, available at specialty grocers under their French name, *haricots verts*, are used, but regular fresh green beans are fine.

MAKES 4 SERVINGS

12 ounces green beans, trimmed

¼ cup extra virgin olive oil

2 tablespoons fresh lemon juice

Salt and freshly ground black pepper to taste

In a large pot of boiling salted water, cook the beans until tender, about 5 minutes. (Or cook them just until crisp-tender; Italians prefer them on the soft side, though not so overcooked as to lose their color.) Drain very well, place on a serving platter, and cool. Just before serving, sprinkle with the oil and lemon juice and season with salt and pepper. Serve hot, warm, or at room temperature.

Olive Oil Note: Use a fragrant, sharp extra virgin olive oil, estate bottled if possible.

Tuscan Bread Salad

PANZANELLA

This is a lovely summer salad from Tuscany. Simple as it is, there are secrets to a good panzanella. First, use only the best, most flavorful tomatoes. Second, choose a very coarse, crusty Italian-style bread, and be sure it is quite firm and stale (at least a day old, two is better), as a soft, fresh bread will disintegrate during the soaking procedure. And finally, use a very good extra virgin oil with plenty of flavor, preferably from Tuscany.

MAKES 8 SERVINGS

1 pound stale coarse Italian or French bread, sliced

1 pound ripe medium tomatoes, seeded and chopped

4 spring onions or scallions, chopped

1 large cucumber, peeled, halved lengthwise, seeds removed with a spoon, and thinly sliced

12 large basil leaves, torn into small pieces

6 arugula leaves, well rinsed and torn into large pieces

¾ cup extra virgin olive oil

3 tablespoons red wine vinegar

Salt and freshly ground black pepper to taste

Soak the bread in a large bowl of cold water until softened, 3 to 5 minutes. Squeeze out all of the water and crumble the bread into a large salad bowl. Add the tomatoes, onions, cucumber, basil, and arugula and toss well. In a medium bowl, whisk together the oil and vinegar, and season with salt and pepper. Pour over the salad, tossing to mix. Serve at room temperature.

Olive Oil Note: Use a good extra virgin olive oil, preferably from Tuscany.

Cauliflower Fried with Garlic and Chile

Parboiled cauliflower that is quickly "passed in a skillet" containing hot olive oil, garlic, and a chile pepper is simple and delicious. Try this method with cooked broccoli as well.

MAKES 6 TO 8 SERVINGS

1 medium cauliflower, cut into florets

¼ cup extra virgin olive oil

4 garlic cloves, minced, or less to taste

1 small dried hot red chile pepper, crumbled

Salt to taste

In a large pot of boiling salted water, cook the cauliflower until just tender, about 8 minutes. Drain very well. In a large skillet, heat the oil over medium heat. Add the garlic and chile pepper and stir until the garlic just colors, about 1 minute. Add the cauliflower and cook, stirring continuously, until completely coated with the aromatic oil, about 2 minutes. Season with salt to taste, then serve immediately.

Olive Oil Note: Use an extra virgin olive oil with a good strong flavor.

Roasted Radicchio

If you can find it, use the long-leafed radicchio from Treviso, in the Veneto, rather than the more familiar round radicchio that looks rather like a small red cabbage. While the round radicchio will work, Treviso radicchio has a less bitter flavor. You can also use Belgian endive.

MAKES 6 SERVINGS

6 small heads radicchio (about 4 ounces each), preferably di Treviso, halved lengthwise

¼ cup extra virgin olive oil

Salt and freshly ground black pepper to taste

Preheat the oven to 400°F. Lightly oil a baking sheet. Place the radicchio on the baking sheet, cut sides up, and drizzle with the oil. Bake for 10 minutes. Turn the radicchio and continue baking until lightly wilted and browned, 7 to 10 minutes longer. Season with salt and pepper and serve immediately.

Olive Oil Note: My first choice would be an extra virgin olive oil from Lake Garda; if it's not readily available, use any good extra virgin olive oil.

Artichokes, Jewish Style

Roman cooking was enriched when, at the unification of Italy, the old Jewish ghetto was opened up and its tasty specialties were introduced into the local traditional fare. These golden brown artichokes are a world apart from the typical boiled variety, mainly because you eat the whole thing, not just the "meat" from the leaves. They are usually served as a first course, but also make an excellent side dish. Make them with small artichokes at the beginning of the season.

MAKES 4 SERVINGS

4 medium artichokes (about 7 ounces each)

1 lemon, halved

Olive oil for deep frying

Salt to taste

Remove the tough outer leaves of 1 of the artichokes. Snap back and discard the outer layers of dark green leaves to reveal the light green cone of tender leaves in the center. Cut off the top inch of the cone. As you work, rub the cut surfaces well with the lemon to prevent discoloring. Place the artichoke upside down on a work surface, and push down firmly, so that the leaves spread out—and the artichoke resembles a water lily. Rub again with the lemon. Using the tip of a small spoon, scoop out the cluster of purple leaves in the center and scrape out the hairy choke. Repeat with the remaining artichokes. Pour enough oil into a deep, heavy saucepan to come to depth of 2 to 3 inches, and heat to 350°F over medium-high heat. (An electric deep fryer does the best job. Follow manufacturer's instructions for temperature.) Fry the artichokes, turning once, until crisp and golden, about 10 minutes. When almost cooked, flick cold water from your fingers over the artichokes, which will help to crisp them. (Be careful! The oil will bubble up and splatter, so be sure your pan isn't too full of oil.) Using tongs, remove the artichokes, letting the excess oil drain back into the skillet, and transfer to paper towels to drain. Sprinkle with salt, then serve immediately.

Olive Oil Note: Use an olive oil suitable for deep frying.

White Beans Cooked in a Flask

This is a recipe for romantics. In some trattorias, where traditional cooking still rules, white beans are stopped up in a Chianti flask (straw casing removed) and nestled in smoldering embers to cook slowly. This method not only produces superior beans, but provides an interesting spectacle for the customers. Pragmatists can use the same seasonings in a pot on top of the stove: Place the soaked and drained beans, the oil, garlic, and bay leaves in the pot, add enough water to cover by one inch, and simmer until the beans are done. Drain and serve.

MAKES 8 SERVINGS

1 cup dried cannellini (white kidney) beans (8 ounces), rinsed and picked over for stones

½ cup extra virgin olive oil

3 garlic cloves, crushed but unpeeled

3 bay leaves

Salt and freshly ground black pepper to taste

Place the beans in a large bowl, add enough cold water to cover by 2 inches, and let soak for at least 8 hours, or overnight. Drain well.

Build a wood fire in a fireplace and let the coals burn down to smoldering embers. Transfer the soaked beans to a 750ml Chianti flask. Add the olive oil, garlic, and bay leaves. Fill the flask three-quarters full of water (about 2½ cups). Tie up a wad of cheesecloth with a long piece of kitchen string, and stuff the cheesecloth in the bottle so that it is only partially stopped up, allowing steam to escape; let the string hang out of the bottle in order to retrieve the cheesecloth. Nestle the flask in the embers, propping it against something sturdy so it won't fall as the embers burn down (being careful not to get ashes in the bottle). Let the beans cook slowly until tender, 1 to 3 hours, depending on the age and dryness of the beans. (Check the flask occasionally; if the water is simmering away too rapidly, add more boiling water and move to a cooler spot near, but not actually in, the embers.) Pull out the cheesecloth. Transfer the beans to a serving dish and season with salt and pepper. Serve hot, warm, or at room temperature.

Olive Oil Note: Use a robust extra virgin olive oil, preferably from Tuscany.

Baked Eggplant, Pizza Style

❧ MELANZANE AL FORNO ALLA PIZZAIOLA ❧

Eggplant is often used to make a substantial main dish in Mediterranean countries, and in the south there are many ingenious ways of ringing the changes. In this recipe small eggplants are used to avoid the bitter juices often found in the larger variety, and the preparation is made even quicker since the eggplant does not need to be fried or grilled in advance. Today it is usually served as a starter, but it can also be served as a main course as it often was in less affluent times.

MAKES 8 FIRST-COURSE SERVINGS,
OR 4 MAIN-COURSE SERVINGS

8 small Italian eggplants (4 ounces), stems removed

6 medium ripe plum tomatoes (about 14 ounces), peeled, seeded, and chopped

3 garlic cloves, minced

1 tablespoon capers, drained and rinsed

8 very thin slices Pecorino Romano cheese (shaved from a large piece of cheese with a cheese plane or swivel vegetable peeler)

1 cup dry white wine

2 tablespoons extra virgin olive oil

3 tablespoons chopped flat-leaf parsley

Salt to taste

Preheat the oven to 375°F. Lightly oil a medium baking dish just large enough to hold the eggplant. Make a deep lengthwise cut down each eggplant so it is almost cut in half. Place the eggplants cut sides up in the prepared dish. In a small bowl, combine the tomatoes, garlic, and capers. Stuff the eggplants with the tomato mixture, then place a slice of cheese, folded in half to fit, in each one. (Don't worry if a little stuffing falls out.) Pour the wine over the eggplant, drizzle with the oil, and sprinkle with the parsley and salt. Cover tightly with aluminum foil and bake until the eggplants are tender when pierced with a knife, about 45 minutes. Serve hot, warm, or at room temperature.

Olive Oil Note: Use a good blended extra virgin olive oil with a mild flavor.

Tender Young Peas in Olive Oil, Florence Style

In spring the market stalls are piled high with mounds of sweet, young peas that are used to enhance plates of pasta, rice, and soup. As a vegetable side dish they are often spiked with small pieces of prosciutto, but I love this simple Tuscan recipe that focuses on the delicate flavor of the young peas. They are so good I often make a meal of them.

MAKES 6 SERVINGS

½ cup extra virgin olive oil

1 medium white onion, thinly sliced

3 cups tender young peas (3 pounds peas in the pod)

Salt and freshly ground white pepper to taste

In a medium skillet, heat the oil over medium-low heat. Add the onion and cook, stirring, until softened but not colored, about 3 minutes. Add the peas and cook, stirring often, until barely tender, about 4 minutes. Season with salt and pepper and serve immediately.

Olive Oil Note: Use a good delicate extra virgin olive oil, preferably Tuscan.

Eggplant Rolls

These eggplant rolls are usually served as a starter, but the quantities can be increased to make a vegetarian main course. Like most Italian eggplant recipes, this one is from southern Italy. Choose eggplants with an elongated, rather than plump, shape.

MAKES 6 SERVINGS

2 medium eggplants (1 pound each)

Coarse (kosher) salt for sprinkling

Olive oil for shallow frying

1 ½ cups Tomato Sauce (see page 40)

Salt and freshly ground black pepper to taste

8 ounces mozzarella cheese, cut into 12 sticks approximately 3 inches long and ¾ inch thick

12 large fresh basil leaves

⅓ cup freshly grated Parmigano-Reggiano cheese

Cut each eggplant lengthwise into 6 slices about ⅓ inch thick, trimming off the round "hump" for the first and last slices from each one. Sprinkle the slices with coarse salt and place in a colander on a plate. Let stand for 1 hour to purge the bitter juices. Rinse the eggplant well and pat dry with paper towels. Working in batches, fry the eggplant slices, turning once, until lightly browned, about 3 minutes. Drain on paper towels.

Preheat the oven to 400°F. Lightly oil a 9- by 13-inch baking dish and pour in half of the tomato sauce. Season the eggplant slices with salt and pepper. Place a mozzarella stick and a basil leaf across one end of each slice, roll up, and place seam side down in the prepared dish. Spread the remaining tomato sauce over the top and sprinkle with the Parmesan cheese. Bake until the sauce is bubbling and the cheese has melted, about 20 minutes. Serve immediately.

 Olive Oil Note: Any good oil works well in this dish.

Potatoes and Zucchini

The southern Italian tradition of creating mouth-watering dishes from simple ingredients is called *cucina povera* ("poor cooking"), a term that refers to the economic status of the original cooks, not the quality of their food. Many of these delicious dishes are vegetarian, as meat was quite expensive, and while we serve this as a side dish, it also makes an excellent vegetarian main course. This is a most versatile recipe in the "poor cooking" canon, sometimes made with trimmed artichokes or eggplant slices instead of the zucchini.

MAKES 6 TO 8 SERVINGS

2 pounds baking potatoes, peeled and sliced into ⅛-inch-thick rounds

2 pounds medium zucchini, scrubbed and sliced into ¼-inch-thick rounds

5 ripe plum tomatoes, peeled and sliced into ⅓-inch-thick rounds

1 medium onion, thinly sliced

½ cup chopped fresh flat-leaf parsley

½ cup freshly grated Pecorino Romano cheese

Salt and freshly ground black pepper to taste

2 tablespoons dried bread crumbs

3 tablespoons extra virgin olive oil

Preheat the oven to 375°F. Lightly oil a 9- by 13-inch baking dish. Layer one third of the potatoes and zucchini in the dish. Top with half of the tomatoes and onion. Sprinkle with half the parsley and 2 tablespoons of the cheese, and season with salt and pepper. Repeat the layering, using half of the remaining potatoes and zucchini and the remaining tomatoes and onion. Sprinkle with the remaining parsley, 2 more tablespoons of cheese, and salt and pepper. Top with remaining potatoes and zucchini, and season again. Pour ½ cup of water into the casserole. Sprinkle the bread crumbs and the remaining ¼ cup cheese over the top and drizzle with the olive oil. Bake until the potatoes are tender, about 1½ hours. Let stand for 5 minutes, then serve hot.

Olive Oil Note: Use a good extra virgin olive oil, preferably from the south.

Desserts

DOLCI

Traditionally an Italian meal concludes with fruit, slices of fennel (in the south), or, at most, a gelato or water ice. Cakes or pastries are eaten as between-meal treats or served to visitors with a glass of sweet wine. Today, however, many light desserts have been "borrowed" from other culinary traditions, and these use Italian fruit in an interesting way. And many cakes and biscuits that originally were made with lard are now being made with olive oil.

Sweet Ricotta Tart with Olive Oil Crust

This dough is very easy to make, resulting in a sweet, crumbly, cookie-like crust that differs from the flaky, butter-based kind. It has the added benefit of not having to be rolled out—it is simply pressed into the tart pan. You will find yourself using it often, but it is particularly lovely with this orange-scented ricotta filling.

MAKES 8 SERVINGS

OLIVE OIL PASTRY

1½ cups all-purpose flour

¼ teaspoon salt

¼ cup plus 1 tablespoon olive oil

⅓ cup iced water, plus more if necessary

RICOTTA FILLING

3 tablespoons pine nuts

2½ cups ricotta cheese

¼ cup sugar

2 large egg yolks

1 tablespoon all-purpose flour

1 tablespoon fresh orange juice

1 tablespoon finely chopped candied orange peel

1 tablespoon golden raisins

Grated zest of ½ large orange

Preheat the oven to 325°F. Lightly oil a 9-inch fluted tart pan with a removable bottom. To make the crust, in a medium bowl, combine the flour and salt. Make a well in the center and pour in the oil and water. Stir until the dough is moist enough to hold together when pinched between the thumb and forefinger. Add a few more droplets of water if necessary. Gather the dough together and press it firmly and evenly into the bottom and up the sides of the prepared pan. Refrigerate while you make the filling.

To make the filling, toast the pine nuts in a small dry skillet over medium heat, stirring often, until lightly golden, about 3 minutes. Transfer to a medium bowl. Add the remaining ingredients and mix well. Pour into the tart shell and place the pan on a baking sheet. Bake until very lightly browned on top, about 1 hour. Cool completely on a wire cake rack, then remove the sides of the pan and serve.

Olive Oil Note: Use a mild, gold-colored olive oil with a neutral flavor.

Olive Oil Puffs with Gorgonzola Filling

&cio; BIGNÈ AL GORGONZOLA &cio;

Once you have prepared a batch of tender *bignè*, you are free to fill them at will with sweet or savory fillings. They are usually made with butter, but olive oil makes them even lighter. These puffs are delicious appetizers to serve with *aperitivi*. In Italy I use twelve ounces of a Gorgonzola and mascarpone cheese torta in the filling. You can find similar tortas in well-stocked American cheese shops, but this version will work with any blue cheese—the mild Italian Gorgonzola, *dolce di latte*, is my first choice.

MAKES ABOUT 4 DOZEN

OLIVE OIL PUFFS

1 cup water

½ cup olive oil

½ teaspoon salt

1 cup all-purpose flour

4 large eggs, at room temperature

1 large egg yolk beaten with 1 teaspoon milk, for glaze

GORGONZOLA FILLING

12 ounces blue-veined cheese, preferably Gorgonzola, at room temperature

⅔ cup finely chopped walnuts

¼ cup plus 2 tablespoons heavy cream

Freshly ground black pepper to taste

Position the racks in the top third and center of the oven and prehcat to 400°F. Lightly oil two large baking sheets. To make the cream puffs, in a deep, narrow saucepan, combine the water, oil, and salt and bring to a boil over medium heat. As soon as the water comes to a boil, remove from the heat and stir in the flour, beating briskly until the mixture forms a smooth ball. Return the pan to low heat and stir constantly until the dough forms a film on the bottom of the pan, about 30 seconds. Remove from the heat and let stand for 5 minutes. Beat in the eggs, one at a time, beating well after each addition (the dough will appear to break up when each egg is added, but will come together with stirring). Transfer the dough to a pastry bag fitted with a ½-inch-wide plain tip and pipe mounds of the dough, about 1 inch wide, onto the baking sheets, spacing them about 1 inch apart. (Or drop the dough by heaping teaspoonfuls onto the baking sheets.) Dip a small pastry brush in the egg yolk glaze and tap down the "tip" of each mound, lightly glazing each one. Bake until the puffs are golden brown, about 15 minutes. With the tip of a small sharp knife, pierce the bottom of the puffs to release steam. Turn off the oven and let the puffs cool in the oven for 15 minutes. (This prevents them from collapsing.) Remove from the oven and cool completely.

To make the filling, in a medium bowl, mash the cheese with the nuts, cream, and pepper. Transfer to a pastry bag fitted with a ½-inch-wide plain tip. Split the puffs, horizontally and pipe the filling inside. If desired, reheat the filled puffs in a preheated 350°F oven just until warmed, about 5 minutes; do not allow to get too hot, or the filling will ooze out.

Olive Oil Note: Use a mild, gold-colored olive oil with a neutral flavor.

Ricotta Fritters

A very delicious, easy sweet from the southern town of Basilicata. You won't be able to make enough of these as they will disappear almost instantly from the plate. Use fresh ricotta cheese if you can find it.

MAKES ABOUT 16

1 pound whole-milk ricotta cheese, preferably fresh

½ cup all-purpose flour

½ cup sugar

3 large eggs

2 tablespoons grappa, brandy, or fruit eau-de-vie

1½ teaspoons grated lemon zest

1½ teaspoons grated orange zest

Olive oil for deep frying

Sugar for sprinkling

Place the ricotta in a sieve set over a bowl and let drain for at least 1 hour. Put the drained ricotta in a medium bowl, and gradually stir in the flour, sugar, eggs, brandy, and lemon and orange zests to make a loose batter. Preheat the oven to 200°F. Pour enough oil into a deep, heavy saucepan to come to a depth of 2 to 3 inches, and heat to 350°F over medium-high heat. (An electric deep fryer does the best job. Follow manufacturer's instructions for temperature.) Slip heaping tablespoons of the batter into the oil, without crowding, and fry, turning once, until golden brown, about 4 minutes. With a slotted spoon, transfer the fritters to a paper towel–lined baking sheet and keep warm in the oven while you fry the remaining fritters. Sprinkle with sugar and serve immediately.

Olive Oil Note: Use any olive oil suitable for deep frying.

Orange Cookies

These crunchy cookies, fragrant with the scent of oranges, are especially welcome when served with a glass of orange liqueur. Along the Amalfi Coast, famous for its fine citrus groves, local families make their own lemon and orange *digestivo* called *limoncello*. It may indeed help the digestion, but with a 95 percent alcohol content, it is not recommended for anyone about to drive along the coastal road, with its steep inclines and hairpin turns!

MAKES ABOUT 3 DOZEN

2 cups all-purpose flour

½ cup sugar

1 teaspoon baking powder

⅛ teaspoon salt

½ cup extra virgin olive oil

1 large egg plus 1 large egg yolk, beaten

2 tablespoons chopped candied orange peel

Grated zest of 1 orange

¼ cup plus 2 tablespoons fresh orange juice

Preheat the oven to 350°F. Lightly brush two baking sheets with olive oil. Sift the flour, sugar, baking powder, and salt together into a small bowl. Add the oil, beaten egg and egg yolk, candied orange peel, orange zest, and juice and stir to make a stiff dough. On a lightly floured work surface, roll out the dough to a ⅓-inch thickness. Using a 2-inch round cutter, cut out cookies and place on the prepared baking sheets. Gather the scraps together, reroll, and cut out more cookies. Continue rolling and cutting out cookies until all the dough is used. Bake until the edges of the cookies are lightly browned, about 15 minutes. Transfer to wire cake racks to cool completely.

Olive Oil Note: Use a fruity extra virgin olive oil.

Fried Cream Custard

These crispy diamonds, with their smooth, creamy interiors, are a popular dessert all over Italy. This particular version comes from Liguria. At dessert time, many Ligurians will offer glasses of their local sweet wine, sciacchetra. There is a lovely custom of making a gift of a bottle of this wine to a newborn babe, and burying the bottle in sand (in order to maintain constant temperature) to mature along with the child.

MAKES 6 SERVINGS

2 cups milk

1 vanilla bean, split lengthwise

6 large egg yolks

½ cup sugar

¼ cup plus 2 tablespoons cornstarch

Grated zest of 1 lemon

2 large egg whites, beaten until foamy

3 cups fresh bread crumbs (from crustless bread)

Olive oil for deep frying

Confectioners' sugar for dusting

Line the bottom of a 12- by 7-inch baking dish with waxed or parchment paper. In a medium, heavy-bottomed saucepan, combine the milk and vanilla bean and bring to a simmer over low heat. Remove from the heat. With the tip of a small sharp knife, scrape the vanilla seeds from the pod into the milk, and discard the pod. In a medium bowl, whisk together the egg yolks, sugar, cornstarch, and lemon zest. Gradually whisk in the hot milk. Return the mixture to the saucepan and cook over low heat, whisking often, until very thick and simmering, about 4 minutes. Pour the custard into the prepared baking dish and let cool to room temperature. Chill until firm, at least 4 hours, or overnight.

Place a large cutting board over the dish, and invert carefully to unmold the custard. Peel off the waxed paper. Cut the custard into 12 elongated diamond shapes about 3½ by 1½ inches. (You will have trimmings, which can also be coated and fried for a cook's snack.) Preheat the oven to 200°F. Pour enough oil into a deep, heavy saucepan to come to a depth of 2 to 3 inches, and heat to 350°F over medium-high heat. (An electric deep fryer does the best job. Follow manufacturer's instructions for temperature.) Working in batches, dip the custard diamonds into the beaten egg whites, then roll in the bread crumbs, patting the crumbs so they adhere, and fry until golden brown, about 5 minutes. Use a slotted spoon to transfer the custards to a paper towel–lined baking sheet and keep warm in the oven while you fry the remaining custards. Dust with confectioners' sugar and serve immediately.

Olive Oil Note: Use an olive oil suitable for deep frying.

Crumbly Cake from Mantua

There are many spellings for this cake from the city of Mantova. This cake, which is almost like a cookie, gets the texture that gives it its name from the cornmeal. You can cut it into wedges (do so while it is still warm and soft from the oven), but it's more fun to serve the whole cake on a platter and let guests break off pieces to nibble with sweet wine or coffee.

MAKES 8 SERVINGS

½ cup sliced blanched almonds

1 cup sugar

2 cups all-purpose flour

1 cup yellow cornmeal, preferably stone ground

¼ teaspoon salt

½ cup plus 2 tablespoons extra virgin olive oil

2 large eggs, beaten

2 tablespoons water

Grated zest of 1 lemon

Preheat the oven to 350°F. Lightly grease a 10-inch springform pan with olive oil and line the bottom with a round of waxed or parchment paper. In a food processor, pulse the almonds with 2 tablespoons of the sugar until the consistency resembles coarse crumbs. In a medium bowl, combine the almonds, flour, cornmeal, the remaining sugar, and the salt and stir to mix. Add the olive oil, eggs, water, and lemon zest and stir well to make a stiff, crumbly dough that holds together when pinched between your thumb and forefinger. Press the dough firmly and evenly into the prepared pan. Bake until the edges of the cake are lightly browned, 30 to 40 minutes. Leave the pan in the turned-off oven to cool completely (keep the oven door propped open). Remove the sides of the pan and serve, letting your guests break off pieces.

Olive Oil Note: Use a fruity extra virgin olive oil.

Stuffed Fig Fritters

FICHI FRITTI

The Sicilian writer Franca Colonna Romano unearthed this recipe in a six-teenth-century cookbook. It is as appetizing now as it was almost four hun-dred years ago. Do plan ahead, as you need figs in two states of ripeness—some just ripe and firm, some overripe and soft—and a ripe, juicy pear. Use either green Kadota or Black Mission figs.

MAKES 6 SERVINGS

12 ripe figs (about 1 ounce each), stems removed

3 very ripe figs (about 1 ounce each), stems removed, peeled, and finely chopped (about ¾ cup)

⅓ cup finely chopped, peeled, and cored ripe pear

¼ cup finely chopped walnuts

1 recipe Yeast Batter (page 25)

Olive oil for deep frying

Sugar for sprinkling

Cut a small, deep cross into the whole figs at the stem end. In a small bowl, mash the chopped figs, pear, and walnuts together with a fork to make a chunky paste. Poke a hole into each whole fig at the cross, and stuff with the pear mixture. (If the figs split, just smooth the stuffing to reform the figs into their original—if plumper—shapes.) Preheat the oven to 200°F. Pour enough oil into a deep, heavy saucepan to come to a depth of 2 to 3 inches, and heat to 350°F over medium-high heat. (An electric deep fryer does the best job. Follow man-ufacturer's instructions for temperature.) Working in batches, dip the stuffed figs in the batter, letting the excess drip back into the bowl. (You will have too much batter, but you need a certain depth to coat the figs properly.) Fry until golden, about 6 minutes. With a slotted spoon, transfer the figs to a paper towel–lined baking sheet and keep warm in the oven while you fry the remaining figs. Sprin-kle with sugar and serve at once.

Olive Oil Note: Use any olive oil suitable for deep frying.

Index